TEDUCATION

TEDUCATION

SELECTED POEMS 1949 – 1999

INTRODUCTION BY GERALD NICOSIA

DRAWINGS BY HERIBERTO COGOLLO

Ted Joans

COFFEE HOUSE PRESS

Coffee House Press is an independent nonprofit literary publisher supported in part by a grant provided by the Minnesota State Arts Board, through an appropriation by the Minnesota State Legislature, and in part by a grant from the National Endowment for the Arts. Significant support has also been provided by the McKnight Foundation; the Star Tribune Foundation; the Lila Wallace-Reader's Digest Fund; the Bush Foundation; Target Stores, Dayton's, and Mervyn's by the Dayton Hudson Foundation; General Mills Foundation; St. Paul Companies; Honeywell Foundation; Patrick and Aimee Bulter Family Foundation; the law firm of Schwegman, Lundberg, Woessner & Kluth, P.A.; and many individual donors. To you and our many readers across the country, we send our thanks for your continuing support.

Coffee House Press books are available to the trade through our primary distributor, Consortium Book Sales & Distribution, 1045 Westgate Drive, Saint Paul, MN 55114. For personal orders, catalogs, or other information, write to: Coffee House Press, 27 North Fourth Street, Suite 400, Minneapolis, MN 55401. Good books are brewing at coffeehousepress.org.

Library of Congress CIP Data
Joans, Ted.
    Teducation : selected poems / Ted Joans.
        p.   cm.
    ISBN 978-1-566-89091-5
    I. Title.
    PS3560.02T43   1999
    811'.54—dc21   99-35464
                                                                CIP

10 9 8 7 6 5 4 3 2 1
first printing / first edition

for
Bird,
Babs,
Bearden,
Basquiat,
and
Brother Bill Traylor
do I dedicate this book

CONTENTS

II. Fertil*eyes* & Fertil*ears*

El Hombre de Mañana
(The Man of Tomorrow)
oil on canvas, 1970

A Lifelong Commitment to Change:
The Literary Non-Career of Ted Joans

by Gerald Nicosia

TED JOANS WRITES POEMS about "colored people," as he puts it, and he draws deeply upon both his African and African American roots, but he does not make a career of being black, and he has spent his life avoiding academia, officialdom, and celebrity of any kind.

During a rare lecture at the University of California, Berkeley, in February, 1999, he explained that he usually "doesn't stop moving" long enough to get stuck in a college lecture hall; and on the streets he is almost completely anonymous, a trait he shared with his famous one-time roommate, jazz great Charlie Parker. In "Ice Freezes Red," one of Joans' many anti-racism poems, he describes himself and two other black men standing on a New York City street corner at 4 AM, too cold to go home to their cheap unheated flat, when "a big shiny car" full of white bigots breezes past them, the men inside yelling:

> HEY NIGGERS!!!
> And they sped on down Seventh Avenue
> As fast as that big shiny car could carry them.
> We stood . . . Silent for want of something to do
> Then we three, me Ted Joans, Basheer Ahmad the Moslem,
> and him, the bird, Charlie Parker . . .
> Yeah we three crossed the cold, cold Sheridan Square
> that cold night and
> headed for Barrow Street to that cold place called home
>
> Because we were no longer cold—not now.
>
> We had been heated up, by hate.
> (pp. 40 – 41)

Like one of his contemporaries, Malcolm X, much of Joans' creative energy comes from his fury at the injustices of society, especially toward minorities and the poor; yet he wants his writing to include not only all of black experience, but all of human experience too, from daily life to the wildest imagination. He recalled that once, during the sixties, he met some young black poets, and all their poems were "dedicated to white racism and white villains." Where, he wondered, were their "love poems . . . poems about bears, about potatoes, or poems about the sense of smell, the sense of taste, or hearing?"

Joans' poetry is enriched by his many points of reference, based on his having lived (in Frank O'Hara's phrase) "as variously as possible." To begin with, his literary inspiration comes from three highly divergent sources. First there was the influence of his greatest mentor, arguably the greatest African American poet of them all, Langston Hughes, whom Joans knew in New York. Hughes made a great many breakthroughs for the black writers who followed him, not the least of which was making use of black spoken language as an authentic idiom for black poetry. Next, there was Joans' immersion in the beat life of Greenwich Village, where he met rebel artists like Kerouac, who were (in Joans' pithy phrase) "neither white nor black." When Joans heard Allen Ginsberg read his long breath line poems, Joans thought he was chanting like a Jewish cantor. Rather than try to imitate him, Joans felt inspired to move in his own direction, which was to write in similar, flowing, rhythmical cadences based on his musician's inside knowledge of jazz. Finally, Joans was irrevocably changed by the writings and vision of French surrealist pioneer André Breton. Perhaps more than any other twentieth century artist, Breton opened the fields of literature inward to the subjective riches of the mind, of the unconscious and dream worlds. Breton's goal was not just to expand man's theoretical horizons, but to bring about a liberation of all aspects of our humanity, to allow human beings to live larger and fuller lives than men had thus far deemed themselves capable of. For a black man born in 1928 and raised in the racist near-South (Cairo, Illinois) during the impoverished 1930s, Breton's ideas lit a fire of hope in Joans that has never died, and which has propelled him on his truly remarkable transcontinental career.

Besides the diversity of his teachers, Joans created for himself a tri-polar life in the physical world, as he endlessly travels between three homes: Africa (principally Timbuktu, in Mali); Europe (principally Paris); and the United States (New York and Seattle). These three venues allow him to play three distinct roles: the universal man of color, in touch with the basic needs and emotions of primitive humanity; the expatriate, honing his intellectual edge against European sophistication; and the American black, son of slaves and prisoner of racism, forever cast upon his own resources of wit, guile, and creativity to forge his own freedom.

In Joans' case, the greatness, grace, and magic of the man's poetry come directly from his own life, and to meet him is surely one of life's extraordinary experiences. I still have many vivid impressions from our first encounter, in poet Neeli Cherkovski's beatnik pad in North Beach, in 1979. Ted exudes an irresistible magnetism, most of which seems to emanate from his own boundless joy and wonder at the state of being alive. He is, to start, one of the world's great raconteurs, and will regale you for hours with stories, jokes, character descriptions, and etymologies from a dozen different countries. I remember sitting across from him in Neeli's cramped kitchen, as Ted explained the African American (and often sexual) origins of expressions such as jazz, juke, funky, and rock 'n' roll. I also remember him holding up one of his books, *Afrodisia*, which had a full frontal nude photo of Ted on the cover, and gleefully taking in our shocked and amazed reactions. Like any good Catholic raised in middle America, I could never be as at ease with my sexuality as this man appeared to be; and the more I got to know Ted, the more I realized how truly comfortable he was (and is) with all aspects of his humanity, including the color of his skin.

You couldn't help but see that this man was having a great time inside his own body, completely enjoying the mental and physical equipment he'd been given, which was pretty much the same as everyone else's. In fact, having just traveled cross-country that day, he was probably a good deal wearier, and he doubtless had less money in his pocket to smooth his way. Yet he made living look easy; or as Erica Jong said of Henry Miller, "everything was cake to him." I am sure

Ted's exuberant confidence—what the Italians call sprezzatura—made all of us in Neeli's flat a little envious that night; and it may well have done the same, in a less beneficent way, to the several generations of critics who have made a habit of ignoring him and his five decades of prolific work.

Ted Joans has been excluded from most of the major literary anthologies of the late twentieth century: Don Allen's *The New American Poetry*, the late sixties blockbuster *Black Voices*, Ann Charters's *The Beat Reader*, and, most ironically, the *Norton Anthology of African American Literature*, edited by Henry Louis Gates, Jr.

"Teducation" refers not to dry classroom instruction but to Joans' genuine desire to share his vast experiences and learning—not scholarly erudition but wisdom gained on his feet, in constant motion—and to share it lovingly and humorously with his readers and listeners, whom he regards as the entire family of man. The best way to read Joans may well be with an almanac and English, French, Spanish, and African American (slang) dictionaries at your side, as he continually forces you to look up obscure place names and words like Tuareg, okapi, and pangolin, to understand jive-talk, and even to translate whole passages from another language. You may think that Joans is a show-off, but the truth is that he works incredibly hard at his craft of poetry just to let you, the reader, into at least a part of the richness of his world.

Breton dubbed Joans "the only African American surrealist." West Coast poet and critic Jack Foley has stated, "Ted Joans is a musician, a surrealist painter, a jazz and surrealist poet, a world traveler, and a filmmaker. He does not write surrealistic poems—it's not like surrealism. He's it! He is the real thing." And for Joans, to be a surrealist means going beyond the tricks of the trade, such as fantastic imagery, "demystified" language (such as words used out of their ordinary contexts), dream exploration, and automatic writing—all of which he does quite well. It means, beyond all that, a lifelong commitment. In his own words: "Surrealism demands, like jazz, a very serious, consistent intellect—and that's the point."

As an example, Joans cites the poem he wrote for Ntozake Shange, "Commonplace Bulues," an erotic poem that (as he puts it) "has nothing to do with touching her." Instead, he gives us a kind of tour-bus ride through his libido: "I want to hang around your kitchen and watch / pots and pans make love to you /. . . I want to lay out on your sofa and watch / Rug and carpet make love to you. . . ." (p. 142) Why is he tickling and teasing us with apparent nonsense instead of saying what he really wants to say? For the same reason, he says, that old-time black men, seeing somebody they never expected, would exclaim: "Well shut my mouth wide-open!" Or as blues singer Bessie Smith sang, "Sitting here wondering, would a matchbox hold my clothes." Just as surrealism aims to give a truth beyond truth, Joans' poetry takes the world we think we live in and gives it a whole new shape, sound, and significance; and this act of transformation adds profoundly to our sense of what it means to be human.

Joans divides this collection into "Hand Grenade" poems and "Fertileyes & Fertilears" poems. Loosely speaking, the "hand grenade" poems are those in his Langston Hughes vein; while the "fertileyes & fertilears" poems come more directly from the influences of Breton and surrealism. For Joans, a hand grenade poem is one that you write immediately out of an urgent situation, such as a human hurt or injustice, that calls for direct action to heal or correct it. The poem explodes against those who have caused the hurt, does its job, and is not necessarily intended to last, though clearly many of them have. In fact, Joans puts the lie to the old saw that political poetry isn't really art. Most of his "angry poems" go far beyond polemicism or pro-grammatic solutions, and get to the core of the cruelty and callous-ness that are, unfortunately, also part of our humanity. But inherent in our natural badness is also a perennial ability to change, and it is to this hopeful possibility that even Joans' angriest poems are directed. As he writes in "Have Gone, Am in Chicago":

> They who ride conveyor-belt train to and fro daily nightly
> Well paid and treated very well these wage-slaves
> They employed at jobs where no pleasure is ever prevailing
> They salute flags kneel before godollar and will murder
> Wage slaves who work for "a living"
> Workers of Chicago Stop Working Unite For Pleasure Work!!

Chicago be different   be a city-poem love and let love
(p. 34)

Another reason these hand grenade poems often reach the level of art is that Joans roots them deeply in his own black ancestry; so that, rather than the Marxist screeds of someone like Amiri Baraka, they read much more like traditional African curses or spells. They can also be hypnotic and incantatory in the manner of an African chant, such as Joans' poem "The Nice Colored Man," in which he takes every permutation of the word *nigger* and turns it into a curse against all racists, ending with the threat: "Eeny Meeny Minee Mo / Catch Whitey By His Throat / If He Says—Nigger / CUT IT!!" (p. 90)

As for his "fertileyes & fertilears" poems, they are the product of an off-beat inventiveness cut loose from every restraint of reason or so-called common sense. They are, as Foley writes, both "brilliantly playful and deeply serious . . . Who but Ted Joans would have transformed the word 'Surrealist' into 'Sure, really I is?' " Joans himself explains the goal of "fertileyes & fertilears" in an early poem called "Let's Play Something": to "create a new life that is an eternal surreal ball / marvelous for yellow ones / black ones / living / sharing / caring and healthy creating /. . . a new hip world where there is hope." (p. 55)

Joans well might have included a third category called "Who else?" poems, for he has written poems on subjects that no other poet I know has tackled: an ode to watermelon; a lovely hymn to the saxophone (What other jazz poet has even tried?); a paean of gratitude to his own bed.

One might add that a good many of his poems are also love poems, not only to women he has loved, like his long-time traveling companion and "femmoiselle" Laura, but also to his mother, to Charlie Parker, and to many of his heroes, such as Louis Armstrong, Malcolm X, Bob Kaufman, and Eldridge Cleaver. In this category fall two of the absolute greatest poems in this collection, and for that matter in Joans' entire oeuvre: the tribute to the elder black literary statesman whose friendship launched his own career, "Passed On Blues: Homage to a Poet"; and the tribute to the handsome young dreadlocked black painter and countercultural hero cut off in his prime by a heroin overdose, another lost African American prince that Joans can only wish to have met: "The Ladder of Basquiat."

As for the homage poem to Langston Hughes, I am not sure any poem in the English language can match it for sheer verbal energy and exuberance. To hear Joans read it aloud is to hear the human voice transformed into a machine gun of pure musical intelligence. Line after line, riff after riff, he captures in short pounding images not only the "world of Langston Hughes" but also the entire black sub-culture both Hughes' and Joans' generations grew out of: "the glad heavy fat screaming song of happy blues"; "the colored newspaper with no good news"; "the cornbread smell, grits, greens, watermelon, spare ribs never refused!" (pp. 66 – 67)

What genius to have written that line, "spare ribs never refused!" For in those four words so much is condensed: a whole generation of black folk who too willingly accepted the privation and oppression foisted on them by white society; but also the openness to life, the readiness to take what is given, however paltry, and find some joy therein, and the power to find both bodily and soul nourishment in the bleakest deserts—traits that have made the black race so strong and admirable throughout the ages.

Likewise, let us not refuse the nourishment Ted Joans herein offers us. It is a rich repast indeed.

Gerald Nicosia,
Corte Madera, California,
August 17, 1999

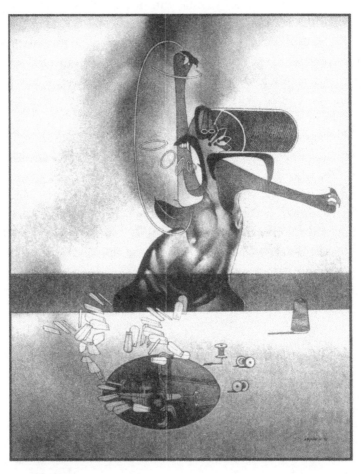

La Rabia de la Costurera
(The Rage of the Couturière)
oil on canvas, 1972

Hand Grenade

GRADED POEMS TO EXPLODE

ON THE ENEMY AND UNHIP

A Few Blue Words to the Wise

to SHOUT / RAVE / RANT / and RAGE   is being militant as
         hell but not very brave
       (Especially when you're before an all-Black audience)

to SCREAM / SNEER / BELLOW / and even fart   is being
         excited / worked-up but
       all that won't stop a Honky heart

to curse / and call him names (all true) is not really bad   Yet it
         makes our black
       poetry look sad (You know, like we ain't got nothing better to
       poet about)

Then: or thus:
We must write poems black brothers about our own black relations
We must fall in love and glorify our beautiful black nation
We must create black images   give the world
       a black education

Africa

Africa I guard your memory
Africa you are in me
My future is your future
Your wounds are my wounds
The funky blues I cook
    are black like you—Africa
Africa my motherland
America is my fatherland
Although I did not choose it to be
Africa you alone can make me free
Africa where the rhinos roam
Where I learned to swing
Before America became my home
Not like a monkey but in my soul
Africa you are the rich with natural gold
Africa I live and study for thee
And through you I shall be free
Someday I'll come back and see
Land of my mothers, where a black god made me
My Africa, your Africa, a free continent to be

An Affair

MONEY MADE

LOVE

TO AMERICA

AMERICA

MARRIED MONEY

AT FIRST BITE

And Then There Were None

the death of Louis Armstrong

AGAIN you have killed another one of us
AGAIN
you have finally overworked the old man to death
you would not allow him to outlive your Picasso
you were always very "fond" of this black man
you never cared whether he was too tired to perform
you and your father and even your grandfather bled him
your musical sons and daughters rode his sounds like parasites
you made a fortune from writing about what you thought he was
you tried to turn him into your "musical golliwog doll"
you wanted his trumpet to blow what you said so
you misinterpreted his wide smile revealing his teeth
you never thought that: Better and Bigger to greet and then EAT you!
you mistook his manners as uncle sam's Tom
you never realized that: Deception was a black style from way back
you never saw him as a powerful black human being
you never heard his trumpet angrier than the Bird, Malcolm, or Trane
you can't quite recall his notes going beyond your "high C"
you forgot that he started very young with a gun
you didn't want to remember why he was born so poor
you never respected him or his artistry like you did You-ropean's
you wished the hell that white lips were so hip and so strong
again you have killed another black brother
this time the world musical giant Louis Armstrong

Animal? No! Cracker? No! Groucho? Yes!

I sing to you
as I bebopped along a song in a perfect late summer August Saturday
noon digging the Soho women's rear ends wagging to and fro here and there
I sing to you
as I am lured into an African art gallery filled with Ngeure masks with
protruding forehead (as though asking a deep question) and seeing the
most beautiful Dan mask in the world suggesting the eternal attraction
of adult/child girls
I sing to you
as the New Morning Bookstore's newspaper screams a headline in a big black
bold type, "GROUCHO IS DEAD," I now sad step and murmur,
        Groucho gone?
I sing to you
for all the Days at Operas / Nights at Races / Yes I mean just that and filled
with Horse Soups / Duck Bizness / and crazy slapstuck Monkey Feathers
I sing to you
your loudmouth brother Harpo wearing the very first Jewfro hairdo to
halo his tightlipped tophat head hoodoo
I sing to you
for all the unlit cigars you held onto, thus sparing your audiences the
wretched cigar stench; your cigar was symbol long before jive Churchill
fatigued Castro and you made demeaning fun at Capitalists cigar mad men
I sing to you
when I need to out talk an indecent dude who is wrong as Margaret
        Dumont
would have been if she be in Harlem 1968 playing her
        haughty-taughty straight
I sing to you
who blew long chain reactions of words as though you'd heard John Coltrane
before he was to be born and Chico did some Monk plunks too
I sing to you
as a true Marxist, but not that dude Karl, but you Groucho, Harpo, Chico,
Marx Brothers who were so social-minded and communal that you took in
        empty Zeppo

I sing to you
for did I not as an infant black tot learn that "new booms sweep clean"
from your 1929 first film *Coconuts?* / and too "why a duck" at the viaduct
I sing to you
in spite of Captain Spaulding copping-out of paying my African brethren who
bore his carcass by colonial hammock chair by land from Africa to Hollywood
I sing to you
as the desk clerk thrice / as the private detective twice / and as the dubious
President of Freedonia whose motorcycle sidecar went nowhere, and too, I
sing to you as the dunce *At The Races* and another dunce in *Go West Young Man*
I sing to you
your oceanliner tiny cabin room with its overcrowded trunk that spewed out
your brothers and then all those other people who filled the cabin until
there was no place for you to do what you had planned to do with
Margaret Dumont
I sing to you
Singing at the university to the weird bearded professors, "What Ever It
Is I'm Against It" and your endless wisecracks, sharp wit that caused the
wealthy bourgeoisie to almost shit / or at least they had a fit causing faint
I sing to you
Mr Firefly / Mr Miller / Mr Kornblow / Mr Driftwood / Mr Hammer /
Mr Flywheel / Prof Wagstaff / Loophole Grunion / Dr Hackenbush /
Quentin Quale / and who else, oh yes,
he is coming, Here Comes Captain Spaulding, Hooray for Cap'n
I sing to you
your bouncing eyebrows / your grease paint moustache / your lensless glasses /
your droopy clothing / your center-parted hair / your leering eyeballs / your
pretentious thumb-in-vest come-on confronting all the imperialists that be
I sing to you
Lydia the tattooed Lady, Lydia, oh yes, I've met Lydia
I sing to you
for the very first, a great classic 1929 *Coconuts* / to the worst 1949
Love Happy
I sing to you
Groucho Marx who attacked it all before the others came
I sing to you Groucho, my eternal movie star

Another Dream Deferred?

a take-off on Langston's famous poem

What happens to a dream deferred?
Langston Hughes poetical said then I read:
Does it dry up like a raisin in the sun . . . etc.
The warm sun the warm winter Mexican sun
Where Aztec executioner priests used to
Make sacrificial blood run
Victims died and all that spilled
Blood dried and dried into obsidian black
In those ancient Aztec times way way back
Did they leave those corpses to fester like sores
To stink like rotten meat
Or did those Aztec sanitation departments
Allow the corpse to just lay there and bloat
In the winter warm sun
Or did they cart hygenically away
Those heavy putrid cadaver loads
Or perhaps they just simply ignored
As many contemporary people by being hard and cold
Who when asked for human help
They just let those living "corpses"' Explode

Mexico City
January 1988

A Powerful Black Starmichael

in memory of Kwame Turé

Senufo mask face . . . . . . You
Torso of kanaga . . . . . . You
Ogun worded mouth . . . . . . You
Kilimanjaro atmosphere . . . . . . You
Elegance similar to an Ellington . . . . You
Lover of the Marvelous . . . . . . You
Yoruba ritual hipster . . . . You
Congo & Chicago chauffeur man . . . . . . You
Afroid acrobat flipster . . . . You
Roaming the world wisely . . . . . . You
Merry Malcolm X-mas every day . . . . . . You
International higher than ladder level . . . . . . You
Cool competent coordinator . . . . You
Ebony Egypt way-a-head Arabs . . . . You
World liberation was what you, yes You were about
You who
Youniversalized power of Blackness

Dakar, Senegal
November 1998

8

Bang Baby Bang

Hey policeman! Why do you carry a gun? to shoot me in the
back if I start to run . . . or is it because you are a frightened man?
Do you go to bed with your woman
with your gun in your hand?
Hey policeman why do you carry a gun? to kill us off if we
don't obey? to mass murder us the legal way . . . or is it
'cause you're a uniformed criminal
and for you crime does pay?
Tell us policeman why do you all carry guns?
can't you enforce the law without a gun?
are you afraid of the public, thus need one?
does a gun give you power of life and death?
Okay policeman I'll carry a gun myself
I'll carry a gun to protect me from you
so when we dispute / we both will know / exactly what to do
Bang baby bang!

Beauty

BEAUTY IS NOT FOUND IN ONE'S FACE / NOR IN THE
    NATIONALITY OF THE RACE
    NO NO WORLD   BEAUTY IS THE SOUL

BEAUTY IS NOT THE DORIS DAY GLITTER / NOR IS IT SAMMY
    DAVIS THAT MAKES YOU TWITTER
    NO NO WORLD   BEAUTY IS THE SOUL

BEAUTY IS NOT THE BLOODY CRY IN BATTLE / NOR IS IT THE
    SLAUGHTER OF BULL FIGHTER'S CATTLE
    NO NO WORLD   BEAUTY IS THE SOUL

BEAUTY IS NOT THE WEIGHT OF MONEY / NOR IS IT A SEX ACT
    WITH A PLAYBOY BUNNY
    NO NO WORLD   BEAUTY IS THE SOUL

BEAUTY IS NOT OWNED BY JUST ONE PERSON / NOR IS IT
    CONFINED TO RELIGIOUS WORDS OR CURSING
    NO NO WORLD   BEAUTY IS THE SOUL

BEAUTY IS NOT THE PAINTING THAT LOOKS SO "for real" / NOR IS
    IT A CORNY RHYMING POETIC DEAL
    (so I shall SHUT UP world) 'CAUSE
    BEAUTY IS THE SOUL

Black February Blood Letting

LUMUMBA WAS MURDERED AND MADE A MARTYR
IN THE MONTH

OF FEBRUARY   BUT NO DISH BROKE IN THE SINK OF THE UN-UNITED
NATIONS

MALCOLM X WAS MURDERED AND MADE A HERO IN
FEBRUARY AND STILL

YET NO ELECTRIC COUCH HAS GAVE BIRTH TO A HIGH
VOLTAGE HUM

ABUBAKA   TAFAWA   BALIWELA   WAS FOUND
DEAD IN HIS OWN
FEBRUARY NIGERIA ALTHOUGH NO WITCH DOCTOR RAISED A BONE
TOWARD MECCA

KWAME NKRUMAH WAS DETHRONED IN HIS ABSENCE
IN THE

GHANA FEBRUARY AND STILL YET I CAN NOT FORGET
THAT NOT ONE:

CHINESE RED RUSSIAN RED OR ANY OTHER
KINDA RED

DID ANYTHING MILITANTLY TO HONOR THESE BLACK
FEBRUARY DEAD

Black Light

It is crystal clear

It is crystal clear to me

It is crystal clear to you

It is crystal clear to them

It is crystal clear to some

It is crystal clear to those

It is crystal clear to these

that we blacks, no longer, want to please

Bread

Money is the world! Dollars / Francs / Marks / Kronor / Pesetas /
Guilder / Rupees / Pounds / Pounds / Escudos / Drachmas /
etc etc Money is your mother / money is your father / money
is your entire family / all your living and dead relatives
mean money / money is your god / money is your god / money is your
god / money is your god / money is your god / your goal is money /
your interest is money / you will cheat to get money / you
will steal to get money / you have always killed to get money /
you have always killed to get money / you have always killed to
get money / you have always killed to get money / you will sell
your soul (if you had one!) for money / you are always looking
for new ways to make more money / you can not have your power
without money / your minutes and years are lived for money / in
the beginning of your life the word was . . . .

Cold

IT'S COLD   CONCRETELY COLD

IN STONE COLD KILLER COLD NYC

AND ME   CAUGHT COLD HAND   IN AMERICA

CAUGHT BETWEEN   COLD RAIN   COLD WIND   AND OLD

COLD FRIENDS   WHO DIG   THEIR AMERICAN

COLD PSYCHIC PAIN   IT'S   SO DAMN   COLD   DAMP DIRTY

COLD   TURNS ME OLD   CUTS MY BLACK BEAUTY AND SOUL

CAUGHT UP   IN THE   FOLD OF   COLD   AMERICA

Colored Choruses

in memory of Bob Thompson

in the window   i saw
the last tear drop fall
crushing a red rose green
glass blades sprinkled
with light white drops
of dew said goodbye mid
night and hello morning blues!

                     trying hard to get it
                     inside (white muse and zem!)
                     where goodtimes roll
                     all night 'n' day long
                     crying loud (white muse)
                     to let you know that
                     I'm (zem) sorry I done
                     you w r o n g !!

Many mother many mothers
point toward others other
and show where the real
truth lies and cries
lies and cries hard
times come fast (if we
last) now that other
many mother satisfies

blow your horn black daddy
scream on the mother for real!
blow your horn black daddy
don't smile   clown   or dance
just
blow your horn black daddy!!

When I saw your face
in the American Express
then I knew your *soul!*

Dead Serious

This was written behind the cotton curtain in the USA while riding in the back seats of a Greyhound Bus.

On the night I first read this in New York some guy told me that it was old fashioned and out of date, but at that precise hour they dragged Mack C. Parker out of jail and lynched him in Poplarville, Mississippi, USA.

When I was young
they said
that I had better
watch out
and I had better not lie
and when I saw a cross
a-burning
that a black man's gonna die
and I'd ask
mama if those sheet wearers
were coming to town

They told me
not to talk to white Cindy Lou
through the fence
like we used to do
and I'd ask
mama if those sheet wearers
were coming to town

One day my dad
talked back to a white
a mob caught him
before he was out of sight
and I asked
mama if those sheet wearers
had come in to town

I remember watching
them tying him to a tree
in this land where
we all supposed to be free
and I asked
mama was them the sheet wearers of our town

I pressed my face to the window pane
and watch 'em beat my dad and pour on gasoline
and I asked mama
was them the real sheet wearers of our town

I had tears in my eyes when they put the
match to his hair
He burned fast like a torch, and they all
laughed and didn't care
and I asked mama
were them sheet wearers representative of our town

I stayed at that window 'til the last
spark on his body went out
I knew he was dead without a doubt
and I asked mama
would them sheet wearers leave town

We buried my burnt dad
in the cold red clay
I swore over his grave
that I'd avenge this someday
and I said goodbye to mama
and I left that town

I came North and went to school
'cause what I was planning I had to be cool
I graduated and joined the Marines
three years there and back on the scene

I caught a Greyhound bus and headed down home
My bags were very heavy
but no toothbrush, clothes, or comb
I got off that bus and kissed my mama
and we headed for our part of town

I noticed ten years hadn't changed much
Nothing built, nothing torn down

I had a big plate of chitlings, corn
bread and sweet potato pie
I glanced at the photo of my dad
and my mama started to cry

For two days I got information
on the old sheet wearers of my town
I knew where they worked and lived
and at what time where they could be found

I worked out my plan on paper
to the last man's fate
I opened my bag, took out some sherry
I decided to celebrate

I cleaned my sniperrifle with regulation care
checked my handgrenades
And other stolen Marine corps gear
And exactly at sunset I kissed Mama
goodnight which I knew was goodbye
I left walking across the fields
under the red sunsetting sky

I dropped the first redneck as he got out his car
The second was killed as he came up a hill
and third and fourth as they sat in a bar
Numbers five, six, seven, and eight

were killed in their bedrooms with their mates
But number nine and ten, who knew
Something was in the wind, went to the
county seat and brought the state troops in
I barricaded myself in the big white kids' school
and sat there waiting for them

They came, two hundred strong, and with a
tank, they were no fools
I got at least thirty, before the tank's cannon got me
but I died happy, happy as one could be, 'cause now
my dad had been avenged, by his son, that's the
    ex-Marine, *me*

Demystify

Don't send me black mail / for I am black male / thus I black ball /
WOMEN / not black sheep / and never black out / awake or sleep / I,
black male / hold black magic secrets / unintegrated thus un-
twisted / whites have black male / as I / delivered censored / or
black listed / I the black male

Domestic Faxophone

Our domestic faxophone rings
There somewhere
Way ahead in advance
Is nobody calling
That wish to be heard
Our number 369 Shit is
An old well paid yesteryear
Lucky lottery number
That Malcom X
Langston Hughes and
Even James Van DerZee
Played them Harlem numbers
Our faxophone rings again
There is no answer
No caller should call
If would not
Wish to be spoken to
Faxophone could answer
But its long paper tongue
Much better like butter
Than margarine outspread
Our faxophone sings thrice
It has a limited patience
Afterwards faxophone's
Voice catcher goes to work
Allowing caller to
Tell the who the how
The where the why the what
And the when—therefore

Our faxophone ears
Are more intelligent
Than the mouths
That contact it
But do not say one word

24 August 1998

Ego-Sippi

i've leaned against the TOWER OF PISA took a piss in the
LOUVRE and laughed at BERLIN in ruins   NOW i read
my poem in 'SIPPI
i've slept between the paws of the SPHINX   wept with joy
at seeing the PYRAMIDS and crossed the SAHARA twice
(alone / stoned / & feeling nice)
NOW I read my poem in 'Sippi
i've lived at TIMBUCTOO / TANGIER / HARLEM / & HAARLEM
HOLLAND too   double crossed the Atlantic which i shall
rename THE AFRICAN OCEAN blue
NOW I read my poem in 'Sippi
and all y'all know that's saying a lot

29 October 1968

Empty Inside Outside

Men who have bald heads
Without one hair remaining
Without any hope of head
Hairs returning should
Count slowly in Chinese
Mandarin up to seven
While wearing seven louder
Than fire engine red ties
As he stands on one foot
At the very bottom of
The world's most loftiest
Barbershop perhaps in
Tibet below a basement
Of couse being video-
Recorded by world TV
To report the hirsute
Miracle condoned by
All the largest religions
In the world who bless
His bold bald head bearded beauty
Empty inside outside

19 May 1992

Faces

I want to see faces

of all races / winning faces / grinning faces / happy
faces / faces that face East in prayer / faces covered & uncovered with
hair / faces up lifted & proud / faces of joy of being in love / faces of
yesterday, today, NOW & tomorrow faces / faces that erased war / faces
that destroyed ignorance, disease, & hunger / faces that faced the tasks
& won / freedom faces / faces of one nation and that nation is the
human being congregation of faces / freedom faces / I
want to see faces / I want to see faces / I want to see faces / I want to
face me

Flutterbye

but
butter
does not
shall not
fly

so fly
your butt
in jet planes
and eat
butter
while flying
and maybe
you will find
a fly
embedded
in your
butter

but
that fly
does not
could not
dig eating butter

it would
perhaps
prefer
your butt
while flying
and so
there is
no such thing
as "butter fly"
but there
has always been
f
l
u
t
t
e
r
b
y
e   s

Yes FLUTTERBYES

3 April 1978

27

Happy 78 Hughes Blues

SO IT IS HERE
WHERE I FLING MY ARMS
LEGS HIGH WIDE AS
THOUGH ENCLOSED NOT
IN FULL FLOWING
BOUBOU ROBE
AND TIS HERE
THAT I TAKE
TO THIS BLUE-BLACK
WARM WINTER SKY
TO SING SWING
ACROSS THIS
POWDER PUFF GREY SUEDE
OF SAND SUN LAND
AS A BIRTHDAY SALUTE
FROM TIMBUKTU
FOR IT IS FEB FIRST
YOUR DATE OF 1902
I SHADOW DANCE NEAR DAWN
HERE IN UPPER AFRICA
WHERE I STAND WITH YOUR BOOK
AND INHERITED LEGACY
ALREADY AT HAND
SO I LEAP OUT THERE
FREE AS A TREE
SAYING HAPPY HUGHES BIRTHDAY
TO YOU LOVELY LANGSTON BLACK LIKE ME!!

Timbuktu
7 February 1978

28

Happy Headgear to They

They very seldom wear hats
when they do apply any form of headgear
be it cap, helmet, scarf, etc it will
inevitably be the colour of shark's tongue
that invariably turn soft compass needles
to opposite direction causing headgear crowning them
to lead the way from poetry temptation

They very seldom wear hats
perhaps their voices are too loud
unless they speak Japanese therefore whatever
is on their heads or minds shall wrestle with
older imagery whilst taking photos from it
similar to a blind dentist with
another hole in the same shoe

They seldom wear hats
wherever they visit annually be they in
Chicago Kinshasa Prague Lima or even Shanghai
if one or two passerby do have something on
their heads it will surely be above their heads
such as an umbrella made of sponges
a thick parasol made of amorous magnifying glasses
or a rather large odorous bar of beauty soap
that emits enormous bright reflecting bubbles

They very seldom wear hats
what few that do have no cavities in their underclothes
and cannot recite second verses of national anthems
or other ridiculous non-erotic chants of control
yet they do preserve stuff blown from their noses
and one wonders do they preserve such waste
when defecating in the privacy of bathing rooms

They very seldom wear hats
one wonders why they do not support a headgear
it could be obvious as a fluttering flag
it could be as blatant as elephant weight
it may be after all that it is too dangerous
deathly as tobacco for them she he her him

They very seldom wear hats
nevertheless one must not ever never suggest
it would be wiser to wear something valid
on their tongues to be covered when or if
a bee ever stung

Harlem to Picasso

Hey PICASSO aren't those Moorish eyes you have
could there be a drop of Africa in your Malaguena soul
Hey PICASSO why'd you drop Greco-Roman &
other academic slop then picked up on my
black ancestors sculptural bebop
Hey PICASSO dig man how did you know
the black thing would make the modern art world
lively / sing   and actively swing
How Did You Know   Huh   PICASSO   PICASSO?

Have Gone, Am in Chicago

On wings of neanderthal dream
Inside this unpretentious no-prop plane
Catapulting itself from nightfilled Newark nest
To thick mattress trunk of blues tree Chicago
Traditional magnetic migratory mouth city
That feeds on those of great needs from the South
The lumber lip black daddy   The timber thin butt white mammy
Dragged along slowly toward the North by their Illinois
Illusions of betterment festoonery too heavy
too worrisome too many pieces of lumpy luggage
All caught up in self-inflicted trick-bag of baggage
Bound for the un-Promising Land
Some with Spanish sprinkled on their greyhound tongue tired
Their border-crossing trailways a weary one
Echoes of early Rio Grande birth warnings: Get back, Go fast, Wetback!
Yet Chicago I have come   Sorry amigo that I ain't you
Up above windowed concrete lanky hut Sears Tower
That awaits criss-crossing clotheslines   to make it world-famous at last
Chicago, fill the entire (including Hancock) building
With the No-Where-to-live tenants especially those that
Sit stagger and illegally upside sleep downtown
House them with their lost iron feathered families and faded armpit friends
Banjo brain white Southern boys   Popcorn picking black ghetto girls
Loafing their luxuriant lives away   Nicotine addicted nobodies
Yet violent opposition to gumdaddies   who lied to become their "leaders"
Chicago, where the saints went marching in
Chicago, where everybody wanted to win on that number
They being unhip to inevitables   Windy City warnings
Chicago is famous for its visible wind   especially winter claw of hawk!
Even founder-settler DuSable·had an electric blanket
When all hells of lakes frown and freeze over all over
Dealing stacks of death on those who
Came to Chicago (sorry it was not just a few!)
The unqualified to be trained and then hired to be first fired

They have settled in the doorways alleys and center city streets
Someday you'll see them dance in the Field Museum great halls
Under the perfect gaze of glass caged natural marvels
This dance will jitterbug you Chicago   Your policemen will flee
The illustrious "scaly anteater" known to pecanpie elite
by its rightful name pangolin
Believe You Me   I Am NOT Who You Think I Am!
There is a road sign on the outskirts of Chicago
That honestly says: Do Not Enter
Chicago icicle ignoramuses in official places know not who
The sacred echidna okapi aardvark or tapir is
Chicago your cretins worship a polluted rainbow authored by
Television telegram telephone and telecomputer
Your unintelligent academic time-passers
remain untold at this late date
To lend a serious consistent ear to Bird Bud Basie Bessie Monk
Yet they dress in woven excrement calling themselves
"the beautiful people" whilst electronic zombies vomit loudly
They would think Billie Holiday was perhaps
Connected to those junkfood motels Horrorday Inn
Chicago there is a giant anteater installed invisible everywhere
Rhinoceroses shall stampede someday soon throughout the city
All your automobiles will die of thirst
Pedestrians shall inherit the streets
Godollar is doomed to play a major rectal role: Toilet tissue
The wind is whispering out loud
Ask any subversive cowrie shell
Better still, go to Gary, Indiana your nextdoor neighbor
Talk to a dead industrial factory
Listen to its crumbling decayed sermon
Grandpapa days of yesteryears shall never be back again
Duke done tol'ya "Things Ain't What They Used to Be"
Remember he, the Ellington one
When Sonny Greer the drummer and chime strummer grinning
Cluttered in an avalanche of percussion Dies & Das
Greer was an ostrich each noon inquire with Nelson Algren
Chicago, where are your "Sophisticated Ladies"

With their brimmed soft hats wearing a ribbon that hums
"Do Nothing Til You Hear From Me"   where they can be watched
Are they deep throat kitchen sinks clad in metal aprons
Are they stomping patient and impatient high heels
Do they speak fluent French-fries behind spinach accent counters
Are they liberated lesbians living in leisure
Disguised as lugubrious huggable housewives
Perhaps they too are entombed in office buildings contemplating
Headline making suicide tonight at noon
O Chicago, you ain't no shy town
Show the world your underground violin-cases machine gun
Sheathed in nippled tip rubber contraceptively secure
Skinback your elevated low-class upperclass consumers
They who ride conveyor-belt train to and fro daily nightly
Well paid and treated very well these wage-slaves
They employed at jobs where no pleasure is ever prevailing
They salute flags kneel before godollar and will murder
Wage slaves who work for "a living"
Workers of Chicago   Stop Working   Unite For Pleasure Work!!
Chicago be different   be a city-poem   love and let love
Yes, have gone to Chicago
And am in Chicago right now
With the bulues   deep summersalty bulues
Chicago when will you be worthy of the six Uli sculptures
That enhance the basement of the Field Museum
Where no two-legged hatefilled greedgut hyena jackal or vulture
They scare your Smokey Bear armed Boy Scouts that witnessed them
Vermin of humanity almost as dangerous as world "leaders"
Draped in old white skins and young black skins
Shame shame shame Chicago Shame!!!
Yes I have gone to Chicago
And my dear honeydrippper   glad not sorry
That   I   didn't   take   you!

Chicago
19 October 1984

34

How Do You Want Yours?

DEAR MR & MRS UNITED STATES   or   GREETINGS   TO YOU ALL
OF AMERICA

YOU IN YOUR COMFORTABLE ALL WHITE OR ALL AMERICAN
NEIGHBORHOOD, suburb, township

HAVE YOU FINISHED HAVING YOUR BALL AT THIRD WORLD'S
EXPENSE?

HAVE YOU TAKEN EVERYTHING FOR WHAT IT WAS WORTH
INCLUDING THIS RETRIBUTION?

[SOFT FLOWERS THAT SMELL DURING THE NIGHT   MOUNTED ON
STEEL FRAMES

WITH R.I.P. AND YOUR NAME   AWAIT YOU FLANKED BY GALLONS
OF GUILT TEARS AND SAD SNOT]

DEAR MR & MRS AMERICA OF YESTERDAY AND TODAY FOR THERE
IS NO MORE GUARANTEE OF YOUR

TOMORROW   THATS WHY YOU AND INSECTS "LONG FOR
YESTERDAY" WHEN, FOR YOU, CRIME DID PAY

ARE YOU READY TO GO?   ARE YOU SICK AND TIRED OF IT ALL?
YOUR GAME IS OVER, YOU LOST!

I GREET YOU WITH A QUICK DEATH IN YOUR HOME OF THE
DEPRAVED LAND OF THE WHITE FREE

THE THIRD WORLD HAS LET YOU SHOW YOUR BLOODSTAINED
HANDS PHYSICAL, MENTALLY GUILTY

[SOFT FLOWERS THAT SMELL DURING THE NIGHT   MOUNTED ON
STEEL FRAMES WITH R.I.P.

AND YOUR NAME   AWAIT YOU   FLANKED BY GALLONS OF
GUILT TEARS AND SAD SNOT]

YOUR TIME IS UP . . . THE KNOCK ON YOUR DOOR IS . . . DEATH
DEATH COMES TO YOU AMERICA

MR & MRS AMERICA WHO ACTIVELY SUPPORTED THE U.S. REPUBLIC
AND FOR WHAT IT STANDS

YOU THE WHITE   OR NEGRO INDIVIDUAL BELIEVER IN THE
    AMERICAN NATION IMPERIALIST HANDS
DEATH IS HERE BEFORE YOU / DEATH IS WHAT YOU NEED   WHAT
    YOU'LL GET / WHAT YOU WERE DESTINED FOR /
DEATH DEATH DEATH / DEATH FOR YOU MR & MRS AMERICA
    DEATH HAS FOUND YOU OUT THROUGH YOU
[SOFT FLOWERS THAT SMELL DURING THE NIGHT MOUNTED ON A
    STEEL FRAME WITH R.I.P. AND
YOUR NAME   AWAIT YOU   FLANKED BY GALLONS OF GUILT TEARS
    AND SAD SNOT]
YOU ARE ALL GOING TO DIE   WHY CRY   YOU ARE ALL GOING TO
    DIE   DEATH IS READY FOR YOU
DEATH HAS ALWAYS HAD YOU AT THE TOP OF THE DEATH LIST
    YOU WILL SOON BE NO MORE
THERES NO REASON TO STAND THERE SMOKING   DEATH AINT
    JOKING YOU ARE GOING TO DIE DIE
[SOFT FLOWERS THAT SMELL DURING THE NIGHT MOUNTED ON
STEEL FRAMES   WITH R.I.P.
AND YOUR NAME AWAIT YOU   FLANKED BY GALLONS OF GUILT
    TEARS AND SAD SNOT]
DEATH CANNOT BE PREVENTED   YOU ARE GOING TO DIE WHITE
    GIRL   YOU ARE GOING TO DIE
WHITE BOY   YOU ARE GOING TO DIE WHITE MAN   YOU ARE GOING
    TO DIE WHITE WOMAN YOU ARE
ALL GOING TO DIE   NEGRO WOMAN TRYING TO LOOK, TALK, AND
    ACT WHITE YOU ARE GOING TO
DIE   NEGRO MAN   WITH YOUR INDIVIDUAL NIGGER MONEY
    GITTING PLAN YOU ARE GOING TO DIE
DEATH IS HERE AS YOU LISTEN TO THIS POEM DEATH IS EACH
    WORD YOU HEAR DEATH SINKS INTO
EARS, YOUR EYES, YOUR ASSHOLE IS FULLA DEATH YOUR SHIT
    SMELLS OF DEATH, SNIFF IT!
DEATH IS INSIDE YOUR DOOMED BODY   YOUR DOOMED WHITE
    SOUL   YOUR TEETH HAVE DEATH

36

BETWEEN THEM SAME AS YOUR TOES   YOUR BONES, PORES,
    BREATH, AND EVEN YOUR SPERM IS
FULLA DEATH DEATH   DEATH INVENTED CIGARETTES TO HURRY
    YOUR DEATH
DEATH CREATED CAPITALISM AND WHITE COMMUNISM TO SPREAD
    DEATH
DEATH MADE YOUR SKIN COLORLESS TO RESEMBLE DEATH
NEGROES THAT LEAN WHITE, LOVE WHITE, WILL HAVE WHITE
    NIGHTS OF DEATH
DEATH DARES YOU TO DROP DEAD BEFORE DEATH
DEATH IS NOT WAITING FOR YOU IN THE DARK BUT IN YOUR
    WHITE LIGHT OF DEATH
YOU ARE ALL GOING TO DIE   YOU ALL GONNA DIE DAMN YOU
    DIE   WHY TRY TO ESCAPE DEATH??
[SOFT FLOWERS THAT SMELL DURING THE NIGHT   MOUNTED ON
    STEEL FRAMES   WITH R.I.P.
AND YOUR NAME   AWAIT   YOU   FLANKED BY GALLONS OF GUILT
    TEARS AND SAD SNOT
DEATH IS GETTING HOLD OF YOUR EMOTIONS / RIGHT NOW / WHILE
    YOU LISTEN TO DEATH
DEATH SMILES AT THE GUILTY 'CAUSE YOU ARE CHILDREN OF
    DEATH   DEATH IS YOUR NATIONAL
WHITE DADDY HE IS FILLED U WITH DEATH / DEATH IS THE MAN
    BEHIND THE COUNTER / WHITE AND
GUILTY OF ROBBERY, EXPLOITATIONS, AND MURDER / DEATH WILL
    GET HIM   DEATH IS AFTER YOU TOO
DEATH IS WITH YOU IN THE MORNING   DEATH IS WITH YOU AT THE
    TABLE   DEATH IS NEVER ALONE
DEATH IS CROWDING IN ON YOU   YOU CAN SNEER AT DEATH
    DEATH DIGS YOUR SNEERS
YOU CAN LAUGH AT DEATH / THAT JUST MAKES DEATH'S JOB
    EASIER   DEATH IS NO LONGER
COMING DEATH IS ALREADY HERE   DEATH IS WITH YOU THE
    GUILTY   THE POET IS THE JUDGE

HEAR THE POETS WORDS   DO THEY SING OR DO THEY STING??
 DEATH IS / IS AND WILL ALWAYS
BE STRICTLY FOR YOU   YOU BROUGHT DEATH TO THE EARTH
 WITH YOUR VICIOUSNESS   YOU
WHO LOVED WAR YOU WHO DESTROYED COLORED PEOPLE   AND
 YOU WHO CONTINUE TO DO SO
DEATH IS YOURS / DEATH IS YOUR TRADITION / DEATH IS THE
 ONLY THING THAT YOU WILL GIVE
AWAY FREELY / DEATH IS ALL YOU NEED   THIS IS YOUR TIME TO
 DIE / DEATH DEATH DEATH
[SOFT FLOWERS THAT SMELL DURING THE NIGHT MOUNTED ON
 STEEL FRAMES   WITH R.I.P.
AND YOUR NAME   AWAIT YOU FLANKED   BY GALLONS OF GUILT
 TEARS AND SAD SNOT]
YOU OF THE WHITE WILL DIE THIS VERY NIGHT / DEATH HAS
 CHOSEN YOU / SO DIE, DIE, DIE, DIE!

Ice Freezes Red

That cold night
When we all hated to say good night
that night when all had frozen
that cold night
when we continued our conversations
just to keep from going to that cold cold room
called home
The cold night when everybody was gone
the cold night when we were all dead broke
Not a dime
That cold night when colder than ever winds blew
We stood trembling and shuffling our bodies
That windy cold cold deserted Sheridan Square night
I remember that night, that cold cold night
when you glanced at the clock
and it was 3:45 AM
My hands were up to my elbows in my pockets
We three stood there in a huddle close together
so as to blow warm breath in our faces as we talked
His breath was reeking of onions
that night the cold night
You had told me about him eating onions and sardines
at midnight, while sitting in the park
in the cold that cold night night
and your breath smelled too
of cheap sweet wine
the type that smells stronger on cold nights
There we stood for more than two hours
Cold and cold and cold all over
but too damn proud to say good night
We talked some and then some more
but never once did we mention "let's go home"
We talked about parties, pot, pussy, pints, and poor

ass pornographic people in perilous public places
We were so cold
Colder than cold
I've always said, that *winter*
was "strictly for whites" only, said he
I have never painted pictures concerning winter and
I never shall! I said, trying to thaw myself out with
laughter
Man you is one cold weather hating cat!
And he is too, he hates cold weather because it brings
hard times, I guess that's why he's a Moslem
abstractly speaking cold weather is down right ridiculous
We three laughed loudly but brief
it was too cold too windy to laugh too long
Yeah we stood there being frozen stiffer by the minute
We talked and shuffled our feet some more
Now we were cold to the marrow of our bones
I asked the Moslem was hell hot or cold. He frowned
and answered, man, you know damn well that hell is cold
We laughed again and blew some more warm breath in our faces
It was so cold so very cold and we were being frozen bit by bit
The winds blew our trouser cuffs they made a strange
flapping noise, that only trouser cuffs can make
It was cold cold cold cold it was so god damn cold!
We talked until 4:15 AM
That cold night at Sheridan Square in cold winter dawn
Then out of nowhere, in a big shiny car, they came
as fast as they could, driving down cobbled Seventh
Avenue fast and noisy. And when they saw us,
they yelled in unison, as they drove by:

HEY NIGGERS !!!

And they sped on down Seventh Avenue
As fast as that big shiny car could carry them
We stood . . . Silent for want of something to do

Then we three, me Ted Joans, Basheer Ahmad the Moslem,
and him, the bird, Charlie Parker . . .
Yeah we three crossed the cold, cold Sheridan Square
that cold night and
headed for Barrow street to that cold place called home

Because we were no longer cold—not now

We had been heated up, by hate

I the Graduate

I graduate
I begin and attend
and finally in time
I graduate
I start at a point
I stay put until
I learn:
   the why / what / how / where / who / and when
and only then
I graduate
Those bridges I don't burn
I graduate
At the top
A much better being
having experienced
That place / person / situation / or thing
N o w   I can swing
I graduate
And move on
Upward again wider and higher
Each time is my first time
I graduated
From my mom's womb
From childhood and family
From neighborhoods
From villages / towns / and cities
From religions / creeds / nationalities
And stagnant allegiances
And fad conformity
I graduated
From it all
I passed the test
I surpassed the exam

I got my paid-dues diploma
It's now mostly deja-vu or deja-done
I graduated
I am no longer a neophyte
I am seriously hip
To that which is seriously happening
I graduated
Although each day
Is the very first phrase of this poem
My marvelous dream surrealized
This poem that money cannot buy
Because I graduated
And since I graduated
My insatiable thirst for personal knowledge
My eternal hunger for shared love
Is rather difficult
In this conventional world
Of unhip undergraduates

I Told On It

I told her toilet
I would tell on it
because it poured giraffe . . .
(Don't Laff!) on me
Now she is beating
that uncouth commode

I told her chair
I would tell on it
because in it
I could not fit
my rhinoceros pet

I told her and she didn't forget
So now she is whipping that bad chair

I told her table
I would tell on it
because it broke
when upon it
I set a half-dozen pangolins
(all from Zaire, and good friends!)
Now she is lashing that low table

I told her radio
I would tell on it
because it sneezed
and no jazz could be found
Now she is kicking that
jiveass radio around

I told her floor
I would tell on it

because it failed to come
to the erection
of A-trainers in
Burundi Alabama
Now she going-up-side
that squareass flat floor's head

I told her bureau
I would tell on it
because it spewed aardvarks
across a freshly painted
chest of dirty drawers
Now she is slapping
that young uppity bureau hard

I told her bed
I would tell on it
because it suggested
white-mailing a certain
promiscuous (already white-listed)
Black mailman from Ghadames
Now she is slugging
that bad mouthing bed ever-whichaway!

I told her ceiling
that I was gonna tell on it
because it got
so high (that I)
at Timbuctu during
camel-racing season
that I couldn't
keep count of okapis
Gnus and Elouises
Got all mixed up
Missed international
pubic publicity and

Harlem hump-back broad
Now she be whupping
that there ceiling's
high be-hind somethin' terrible

I told her bookcase
I would tell on it
'Cause it done done
Number two and won
Three cheetahs six
Tanzanian hours before
five dark clouds
poured (like toilet) giraffe
on my sandy Black books
on my dusty dictionaries
and Charlie Parker recordings!

I told her stove
I would tell on it
in spite of it being
red (hot!) and fulla
laughs inspite of Karl
mixed in with the true
brothers   I told her   !
Now she jumping up and down
on that pot-bellied stove

I told her lamp
I would tell on it
because if squirted
bolts of lightning
that caused my cornbread
to melt in crocodile's
oven mouth
Now she be hell-raising
all across that lamp

I told her rug
I was really going
to tell the whole-wide-
eyed-world on it!
For it had imitated a boa
rolling itself uptight
at the north / south / east
& western edges thus
causing cats like me to burp

I told her window
I would tell on it
because out of it
I could not get
my Zambian elephant yet
Now she is smashing
all the big windows

I told her door
I would tell on it
when it refused
to open and close
for all people
of all colors
at all hours
all over the world
where doors are used
Now she doesn't act
It's the only
thing she has
that she will
not punish or abuse

12 June 1972

Jazz Is . . .

dedicated to Cecil Taylor

a scream / can scare / awake or shake one UP!!
to joy's highest pitch / forth deep into fathoms where / boss
bass sounds rumble / round riffs repeat rhythms / there. . . . .
a shout is what / that's about / five or groove / right on
across the bridge / work and rework them changes / catch
this bit / here   not   steady / ready? accidentally fell in
and out of those fast changing bars / discovering and
uncovering / dare a devil phrases / skipping the last
measure at last minute / plenty plenty soul stirred down in
it in it in it / git up git up / let up off that there click /
away heres what I gotta say / forcing fierce fragments /
out side of me into machine voice / tearing away its
mathematice of so-called so believed and preached music /
a moan may cause tears / reminds or just shatters / the
mask is down on its knees / now to disguise the non melody
in me / out of me / free / glad to be / keep in touch with
your axe / truth streaming across the earth / worming its
way / out beyond the seas / mountains / fields / and grave-
yard giggles / sad at first burst / bigger blacker blacks
to be had / biggest barriers broken / sound pounding is
swings / let freedom swing one more again / bright
explosions hammer human hang-ups dark moods massage
the guilt / gas leak of pleasure / marvelous images
surround / brain tissues / discarding manmade forbidden
issues / these beats blending and bending / back to black /
and forth to forward march / beats heat increased / to
arouse what's really there / down inside / soul sacks / a
black sound / a black sound / leaps / or glides / into the
ear / of the digger (a listener who stirs) and like water and
air / Jazz is . . . . .

good for the soul

Jazz Is My Religion

Jazz is my religion   and it alone do I dig   the jazz clubs are
my house of worship   and sometimes the concert halls   but some
holy places are too commercial (like churches)   so I don't dig the
sermons there   I buy jazz sides to dig in solitude   Like man / Harlem,
Harlem USA Used to be a jazz heaven where most of the jazz
sermons were preached   but now-a-days due to chacha cha and
rotten rock'n'roll alotta good jazzmen have sold their souls   but jazz
is still my religion   because I know and feel the message it brings
like Reverend Dizzy Gillespie / Brother Bird and Basie / Uncle
Armstrong / Minister Monk / Deacon Miles Davis / Rector Rollins /
Priest Ellington / His Funkness Horace Silver / and the great
John COLTRANE   and Cecil Taylor · They Preach A Sermon
That Always Swings!!   Yeah jazz is MY religion   Jazz is my story
it was my mom's and pop's   and their moms and pops from the
days of Buddy Bolden who swung them blues to Charlie Parker and
Ornette Coleman's extension of Bebop   Yeah jazz is my religion
Jazz is a unique musical religion the sermons spread happiness and
joy   to be able to dig and swing inside   what a wonderful feeling
jazz is / YEAH BOY!! JAZZ is my religion and dig this: it wasn't for
us to choose because they created it for a damn good reason   as   a
weapon to battle our blues! JAZZ is my religion   and its
international   all the   way   JAZZ is just an Afroamerican music
and like us it's here to stay   So remember that JAZZ is my religion
but it can be your religion too but JAZZ is a truth that   is always
black and blue   Halleluiah I love JAZZ so   Halleluiah I dig JAZZ so
Yeah JAZZ   IS   MY   RELIGION

J.F.K.* Blues
*Just for Kicks

Because of him there is a fire burning in an Alaskan igloo tonight
Because of him there is a freedom bus smashing the wall of East Berlin
Because of him there will always be a guilty expression on faces from Dallas

So if he is dead . . . . . . Oh No oh no oh no!

Because of him there is a TV antenna on Uncle Tom's splitlevel cabin
Because of him the world waits for Godot and pennies from heaven ·
Because of him Federal stars fell on Alabama to allow Martin Luther King
to ride a bus up front

So if he is dead . . . . . . Oh No oh no oh no!

Because of him U.S. passports are now the color of Caroline's innocent eyes
Because of him rhinoceroses are riding jetplanes to Japan and Holland
Because of him American spades dug deeper into their fight (day &
night) against Southern segregation & Northern discrimination

So if he is dead . . . . . . Oh No oh no oh no!

Because of him tears and laughter stream down between the breast of a glove
Because of him the entire American nation swings back and forward in
a rocking chair
Because of him mighty powerful planes with mega-ton bombs are singing
peace is our profession

So if he is dead . . . . Oh No oh no oh no!

Because of him mad men, mad dogs and high pressure fire hoses
"had" to go down by the riverside
Because of him young Europe looked toward the U.S. for leadership
Because of him millions of Americans read faster and poets get a little
more respect

So if he is dead . . . . Oh No oh no oh no!

Because of him a nuclear testban "almost" banned that damn bomb
Because of him Red China called Red Russia an un-Marxist mother fucker!
Because of him many men parted their hair but kept their wives a little longer

So if he is dead . . . . Oh No oh no oh no!

Because of him Cuban cigars and Cuban sugar are now Cuban cigars
    and Cuban sugar
Because of him culture became the thing in the USA and didn't
    Pop Art start!
Because of him for the first time in U.S. history jazz was played in
    the White House
Because of him new frontiers were started with that All-American "vigah"
Because of him Africa and Asia took their well timed GIANT steps
Because of him this generation was led by the youth
Because of him all the world's politicians had to tell somebody the truth
Because of him there is a growing passion for democracy and peace
    has become the ambition of practically all of mankind

So if he is really dead . . . . . Then I ask you to bow your head and cry
Oh No   Oh No   OH NO!

Le Fou de Bamba

Oh chained human being of Bamba
with your turned up truth exposed
far all the world to see that pass
your Bamba sand dunes crashing Nigeriver
Oh fou Oh crazy (?) man of Bamba
hobbling in chains muttering denunciations
while on dusty shelves Mao,
Marx, Lenin and more Reds lie
unread by those as you uninterested and unfed
Oh chained human being of Bamba
they say you're faster than a gazelle
this Bamba boatstop invades your private purity
thus you wade in the water shoving slim pirogues aside
walking on water to get your crumbs
braver than six hydrogen bomb pushers
soul cleaner than a child's navel
Oh Fou of Bamba
you who fear not
you who have no hangups and no blood on your brow
we are brothers
fou de Bamba fou du Mali
we two know where they are
and we two must break your chains together

Let's Play Something

(to hip humans)

LET'S PLAY SOMETHING   let's play anything   let's play something
let's play that we are all children again watch too much television put
nasty things into our mouths eat too much SWEETSTUFFS wish to
run away from our parents and you show me YOURS and I'll show
you MINE

LET'S PLAY SOMETHING let's play anything let's play something
let's play something serious yes let's play that we are all serious bizness
men and women and we have a very serious occupation and let's play
that we seriously believe that this is serious the work we do the flag
we salute and be seriously all day all night

LET'S PLAY SOMETHING let's play anything let's play something
let's play something daring like going to NYC Central Park after
twelve midnight and strip / then roam around there naked / wearing
nothing but a smile and of course piss on anyone we encounter

LET'S PLAY SOMETHING let's play anything let's play something
let's play Hollywood yes let's make a horror movie a real horror movie
You be Hitler You be Stalin You be Mussolini and I'll be the monster
The Idiot, a mean Dada manufactured by Israel / England for Uganda
let's play something let's play that we are military maniacs

LET'S PLAY SOMETHING let's play anything let's play something
let's play something super cool fool let's play that we are: Far Out Too
Much and use the word WOW and hitch-hike from Marrakesh to
Katmandou and count all our travelers cheques in Hammerfest and
listen to Pop maufactured music as loud as loud as loud as loud!

LET'S PLAY SOMETHING let's play anything let's play something
let's play something sexy yeah let's get into something let's all play
something SEXY like getting into bed but dressed complete even
wearing an overcoat and elbow length gloves and then try to fuck

through all that clothing and give a prize to the first one that has a climax without physical contact yeah let's play that

LET'S PLAY SOMETHING let's play anything let's play something let's play something personally dangerous / physically deadly / and thus very very square and let's try hard to forget that heart disease / cancer and stroke is found in every bit of cigarette tobacco you smoke And let's continue cigarette smoking thus we are unhip and therefore continue to deny that the safest thing to smoke: pot will always get U-Hi!

LET'S PLAY SOMETHING let's play anything let's play something let's play SAFE everybody wants to play safe / let's play that we all play safe by working at a job that we do not enjoy that we do not enjoy and we all work at this (that we do NOT enjoy) from nine o'clock in the morning until five o'clock in the evening / From nine AM until five PM from nine until five from nine until five from nine 'til five from nine 'til five thus we are caught up in the ratrace the ridiculous de-humanizing ratrace because we are trying to pay for those so-called rewards: security and comforts offered by those serious lifetime jobs thus we have to forever be confronted and assaulted by those never ending payments those never ending payments those never ending payments those never ending payments those never ending payments and owe our lives forever!

LET'S PLAY SOMETHING LET'S PLAY ANYTHING LET'S PLAY SOMETHING SOMETHING THAT is the very best / let's denounce all the jive and popular slop / and avoid the controlled programmed de-humanizing mess / LET'S PLAY THAT WE ALL HIP, very hip and wise / thus we are hipsters and hipstresses / we use machinery and do not allow the machinery to use or mis-use us / as hipsters we are spiritually involved with life / and we dig good food / good sex / and the finest of arts and we travel all over this wonderful world / for the entire earth is ours / we love those whom wished to be loved / we kiss but do not kill / we work at jobs that give us thrills / we abuse all money / and we pick up on all knowldege that we can use / we experience all great kicks / we avoid conformity / disaffiliated with any organized goof / thus digging freedom / freedom / freedom now / freedom for all / and create a new life that is an eternal surreal ball / marvelous for yellow ones / black ones / living / sharing / caring and healthy creating / a new hip world where nobody is hungry   where nobody is oppressed   and where there is hope

YEAH LADIES AND GENTLEMEN BOYS AND GIRLS LET'S PLAY THAT YES LET'S PLAY THAT FOR REAL LET'S PLAY THAT WE ARE ALL HIPSTERS AND REALLY BEGIN TO LIVE!!

NYC
1958, revised 1979

Like Me

They ask: what is Africa like? I tell them: Africa is like me ! Black /

Big / complex / creative / magic / undeveloped wealth / and not yet free

Long Gone Lover Blues

WHERE WAS YOUR LOVER WHEN THE SAD SAD SUN
                    WENT DOWN??

WHERE WAS YOUR LOVER WHEN THE BAD BAD MAN
                    CAME AROUND?

THE SUN LEFT YOU IN THE DARK, and the bad man spit on your

heart! SO WHERE WAS YOUR LOVER THAT DAY???????????

WHERE WAS YOUR LOVER WHO KNEW WHAT TO DO
                    IN YOUR BED?

WHERE WAS YOUR LOVER WHO KNEW HOW TO PUMP LIFE
                    IN THE DEAD?

YOUR BED WAS EMPTY AND COLD from making love with your body
and no soul SO WHERE HAS YOUR LOVER DON' GONE?
WHERE WAS YOUR LOVER WHY DID HE LEAVE YOU SO FAST?
WHERE WAS YOUR LOVER WHO HELPED CHANGE
                    YOUR UGLY PAST?
I HEARD HE IS DOWN SOUTH WITH A SMILE ON HIS MOUTH AND
the sun shines bright on him all the day long . . . I heard he
is down south with a smile on his mouth and the sun shines
bright on him all the day long. . . . . . .
                    YES I HEARD HE'S
DOWN SOUTH WITH A SMILE ON HIS MOUTH
                    AND THE SUN
SHINES BRIGHT ON HIM ALL THE DAY LONG!!!!!!!!!!!!!!!

Lumumba Lives Lumumba Lives!!

FOR HE   LUMUMBA   PERHAPS   LUMUMBA   LIKE THEIR
        JOHNBROWN MADE HASTY HURRY UPS

FOR HIS   LUMUMBA   PEOPLE OF   LUMUMBA   BLACK
        AFRICA   WOKE UP ABRUPTLY

SO HE LUMUMBA ON PERHAPS ABE LINCOLN'S BIRTHDAY
        LUMUMBA WAS MADE   A   MARTYR

AND
   NOW   LUMUMBA   SHALL LIVE   FOREVER
IN THE BLACK   IN THE WHITE   IN THE YELLOW   AND IN THE RED
        FOR THESE
PEOPLE KNOW THAT PATRICE LUMUMBA   IS   NOT   DEAD!
LUMUMBA LIVES LUMUMBA LIVES LUMUMBA LIVES!
LUMUMBA LIVES LUMUMBA LIVES!!

My Ace of Spades

MALCOLM X spoke to me & sounded you
   Malcom X said this to me, then told you that
   Malcom X whispered in my ears but screamed on you
   Malcom X praised me and thus condemned you
   Malcom X smiled at me and sneered at you
   Malcom X covered me and exposed you
   Malcom X made me PROUD and you all got scared
   Malcom X told me to hurry and you begin to worry
   Malcom X sung to me but growled at you
   Malcom X freed me and frightened you
   Malcom X told it like it *damn shor* is!
   He said I gotta fight to be really FREE
      Malcolm X told both of us
        the truth, now didn't he?

My Bag

MY BAG   IS HERE   IT IS JUST MY SIZE
MY BAG IS DEEP   AND DARK   SO DON'T
BE TOO SMART   I HAVE MY BAG
IT IS ALL MY OWN   AND I   AND I ALONE
KNOWS WHAT IS HAPPENING IN MY BAG
MY BAG IS WARM SOMETIMES HOT BUT HIP
MY BAG IS NOTHING MORE THAN MY BAG
THUS IT MAY JUST BE TOO DAMN HEAVY
FOR YOU TO WORRY OR TRY TO CARRY BUT
DONT GET UPSET AND SCARY   IT'S MY BAG
I KNOW MY BAG   'CAUSE IT IS MY BAG
I KNOW EXACTLY WHERE IT'S AT   MY BAG

Natural

thick lips / natural
wide nose / natural
kinky hair / natural
brown eyes / natural
w i d e   s m i l e / natural
black skin / natural
& if you're proud / of what you
naturally got
then your soul / is beautiful / thus
naturally hot   so be natural
stay natural   swing natural   think natural
and for black god's sake   act   natural

Harlem, NYC
5 December 1968

Nitty Gritty

Hey moon faced female with your under wear on upside down!!
Why do you have so much kinky hair . . . between your fat legs?
I know what you're thinking   I have been drinking! No you're wrong
I happy loud and crude   When I open my mouth I just sound rude
Hey brownface gal and pale face bitch! I want to go to
                                                    bed with you!
I'm rough and ready *I won't sleep with you* nor let you get *any sleep*
I am a city cowboy that rides women instead of horses and sheep
Call the police I don't give a damn they'll give us some rubbers!
Dial the phone backwards bitch and you'll get god!
take off your clothes baby . . . I want to really see you!
I feel for you so now I am feeling good Rape you with my eyes!
skin back a banana for me baby! Lets get hi!
I'll light a joint while you powder your hole with gold dust
Tomorrow I'm gonna marry your mother
Then you two will have me in the family
Each day and night I'll make everything all right
Did you hear what I said. . . . Now tell me what did I say?

No Mad Talk

AT TIMES ME FEEL LIKE ME JES BACK FROM
      ANOTHER MOTHER PLANET
'CAUSE WHEN ME TALK / ABOUT ME WALK / IN
      MOTHERLAND AFRICA
from TANGEIRS to ALGEIRS / from OUAGADOUGOU to
      TIMBUCTOO / from
ABIDJAN to KAIROUAN / from TRIPOLI to WADIDI or
      to a place called TIT!
Dey look at me real dumb ME WANTA SHOUT "AW SHIT"
      YET INSTEAD
I PLEAD HOPING THAT MY BROTHERS ABOUT AFRICA *DO*
PLEASE READ! 'CAUSE ME NOT A MAN FROM OUTER
      SPACE ME JUST BEEN TRAVELING
AMONG OUT BEAUTIFUL AFROID RACE from TANGEIRS
      to ALGEIRS / OUGADOUGOU to
TIMBUCTOO / ABIDJAN to KAIROUAN / ACCRA to DAKAR /
      CONAKRY to MOPTI / BAMAKO to
KANO / TIZNIT to TESSALIT / MEKNES to AGADES /
      BANGUI to BENGHAZI / CAIRO to
BOB-DIOLASSO / MOMBASA to KINSHASA / IFE to GOREE
      KORHOGO to OSHOGBA
Happy New Year in TIMIMOUM
and suddenly Sudan's KHARTOUM
from Madagascar's ANTANANARIVO
to Mozambique's MAPUTO
—and to a place in MOROCCO
      called TIT!

O Great Black Masque

O great black masque   that is me
that travels with me in spirit
your big eyes that see tomorrows
saw yesterdays   and gazes at now
O great black masque of my soul
those ears have heard the clink
of slaves chains   and the moans
of sorrow   of our past   but those
same ears   can hear our now
O great black masque   that is   me
you who copulated with Europe's science
and now dynamically demystifies Europe
O great black masque   who is our
ancestors   with your cave mouth
filled with sharp teeth   to chew
the ropes that bind our hands and minds
O great black masque   you that grins
you that always wins   the thrower of
seven cowries   and two black-eyed dice
O great black masque   who says that it
half past pink since white is not a color
O great black masque   that carried me from Bouake
to Alabama and back   From Mali to Manhattan
O great black masque that dances in me day and night
O black maque of urban guerillas and forest gorillas
O black masque that screams in joy at childbirth and
opens up to the rays of the sun   O great black masque
your sharp blade tongue burns war makers buildings
You who stand guard to African breast and soul
O great black masque give us our blacker heavens /
release our minds from borrowed white hells / O great
black masque of Africa   O great black masque of all
black people   O beautiful black masque Our own black
truth

Passed On Blues: Homage to a Poet

the sound of black music
the sad soft low moan of jazz ROUND BOUT MIDNIGHT
the glad heavy fat screaming song of happy blues
That was the world of Langston Hughes

the mood indigo candle flame
the rough racy hot gut bucket riff tune AFTER. HOURS
the fast swinging rapid rocking riff rumping blues
That was the world of Langston Hughes

the funky butt grind
the every night jitterbug jiving gliding his TROUBLE IN MIND
the brown black beige high yaller bouncer's shoes
That was the world of Langston Hughes

the sonata of Harlem
the concerto to shoulder bones / pinto beans / hamhocks IN THE DARK
the slow good bouncing grooves
That was the world of Langston Hughes

the elephant laugh
the rain forest giggles under a switchblade downpour
the zoot suited conked head razor throat STOMPIN' AT THE SAVOY
the colored newspaper with no good news
That was the world of Langston Hughes

the Jess B. Semple hip sneer
the bassist / drummer / pianist / guitarist / rhythm on top of CALDONIA
the take it, shake it, rattle, lay back & make it (or lose!)
That was the world of Langston Hughes

the big black mouth
the pawnshop / butcher shop / likker shop / . . . BEBOP!
The rats in the rice, roaches of reefers on relief amused
That was the world of Langston Hughes

the Manhattan subway stool
the naked thigh, double-breasted one-button ROLL ON TO JESUS!
The poolroom chalk & click, fat chick wobble in cigarette tar baby crews
That was the world of Langston Hughes

the chain gang jingle
the evil laughter against the atomic HONEYDRIPPER
the brownstone tenement cold filthy frozen winter hell ghetto dues
That was the world of Langston Hughes

the uh-huh, Oo-wee, oh yeah of hot climax
the hustlers haunt, prostitutes pimp, bitter SWEET GEORGIA BROWN
the hep hip hi junkie tongue tied black-eyed bruise
That was the world of Langston Hughes

the sounds of dangerous black humor
the swift sharp flash of Afroamerica STRUTTIN' WID SUM BAR-B-Q
the *Presence Africaine,* Harlem Jew, chittlin switching cruise
That was the world of Langston Hughes

the fried fish 'n' chicken boogie-woogie
the storefront church Cadillac / wigwearing / gospel truths / WHEN
    THEY CRUCIFIED MY LORD
the nigger-loving Thirties, dozens by the dirties on ofay's muse
That was the world of Langston Hughes

the rent party good-timing crowd
the shout strut twist turning loud raving but AIN'T MISBEHAVIN'
the darkie, jig, coon, hidden shadowy shadowy spade drowned in
    booze
That was the world of Langston Hughes

the taker of A TRAINS
the sticker upper, alley cat, hustler, poolshark cleanhead HUCKLEBUCK
the cornbread smell, grits, greens, watermelon, spare ribs never refused!
That was the world of Langston Hughes

the cool crowded summer solo horn
the red rattled raisin around the sun / migrated Dixieland STRANGE
      FRUIT
the jim crow / black crow / Ol' Crow / moonshine splo / niggers
      can't go or choose
That was the world of Langston Hughes

the sweaty hard working muscle-making black back-breaking hard
      labor hump
the bold bright colors on ebony nappy-head big-titty itty-bitty Liza Jane
the millions and millions raising-up-strong been-done-wrong
      too-long pointing
the abused body at slumlord! War lord! Police lord! Oh Lord, all
      guilty and accused!
THAT WAS THE WORLD OF THE POET LANGSTON HUGHES
    BLACK DUES! BLACK BLUES! BLACK NEWS!
THAT WAS THE WORLD OF THE GREATEST BLACK POET
      LANGSTON HUGHES

Poet Key

Yes we walk   talk to ourselves
Not because   we are alone   for
This place is crowded   with prisoners
Some are lifers   most are insane
Yet amongst the "crazy ones"
There is a   poet   or two: see he!!   hear her?
Yes we walk   talk to ourselves
So there is hope   here if they
Who do not know how   to be cool
Would listen   to our loud whispers
Could be inspired   by her poem sigh
Then within   a tiny time   prison
Would be   completely destroyed with
An all together poet-key   in harmony

Paris
26 April 1979

Promised Land

LANGSTON HUGHES
PAID HIS DUES
IN THE HARLEMS
OF   THE   USA
HE
POETED THE
POLLUTED
MAKING PROSE
TO   ZOOT   SUITED
THUS   TOLD WHAT
THE   NEGRO
HAD   TO SAY
LANGSTON HUGHES
NEVER   BLEW   HIS   COOL
NOR DID HE
SIDE   WITH
THE "MAN"
HIS STORIES, PLAYS &
PROSE
& HIS BLACK POETRY
SHOWS
NIGGERS CAN'T
WAIT
FOR NO
"PROMISED LAND"

Repression

The gate will shut soon
the wall will become a square
the openings will be no more.
only the sky will be wide (outside)
only the clouds will hover
the landscape will be abrupt
the vision shortsighted
the miles only an inch or two
the space is only before the nose
the air is that which fills your lungs
the sky is cloudless now
the color of the sky is gone
the sky's heaviness hangs above
the ceiling is this thick sky
only thick sky could be the lid
the gate has shut on all sides
this place is now a prison

Salute to the Sahara

Sahara I have crossed you
with four liters of water
oriental patience and
ancestral spiritual guidance
I dreamed I had two Swiss cooks
who pushed a Volkswagen bus
across your vast seas of sand and rock
I salute you Sahara   you've always frightened
Western man   who thinks you're nothing but an
ocean of sand   I know what you are I've traveled you
triple sunsets / more welcome dawns / hot high noons
You are a big brown woman with legs spread wide
waiting for the masculine and brave to come inside
I salute you Sahara   the mighty / the dangerous / Sahara

Sanctified Rhino

The rhinos roam in the bedroom
where the lovely virgin waits
the owl eats a Baptist bat
and God Almighty is too late

The statutory chicklet's mommie
was wrestling with the future bright
the ol' hound dog of blues hollow log
cried and howled in the still of night

The rhino roots a baby goose
while the marvelous candles glow
the owl howls the Ginsberg address
that only the hipster would know

The statutory chicklet's dreams
frilled with H-bomb-age hopes
the motorcycle rider sat down besid'er
her only answers: twelve nopes

The rhino runs with the virgin
which caused her halo to slip
the owl was digging, this chick's wigging
so the rhino kissed her on the lips

The rhino and virgin standing
where once lived a preacher cat
a Swahili instructor, tried to make her
she ran away with a dish and a bat

The rhino and his two head horns
went to sleep on a purple pillow bed
Baby goose came twice, and broke the ice
and rhino gave her his head

Now statutory chicklet has a trophy
hanging over her used fireplace
like jazz is her religion
so the philosopher can't state her case

She has become independent
like the owl who ate Baptist bat
the rhino knows, and he shows
the relationship stays as that

So the rhino who balled the virgin
on the twelve o' clock saturday bright
blew his horn, for she was reborn
on wines, made 'em high as a kite

Now rhino preaching in wilderness
about how he lost his great head
by talking, and walking baby goose
virgin to his purple pillow bed

And that's how he lost his head
by taking and shaking baby goose
the virgin to his purple pillow bed.

1956

Santa Claws

IF THAT WHITE MOTHER HUBBARD COMES DOWN MY BLACK
    CHIMNEY   DRAGGING HIS PLAYFUL BAG
IF THAT RED SUITED FAGGOT STARTS HO HO HOING ON MY
    ROOFTOP
IF THAT OLD FAT CRACKER CREEPS INTO MY HOUSE
IF THAT ANTIQUE REINDEER RAPER RACES ACROSS MY LAWN
IF THAT OLD TIME NIGGER KNOCKER FILLS MY WIFE'S STOCKING
IF THAT HAINT WHO THINKS HE'S A SAINT
COMES SLED FLYING ACROSS MY HOME
IF THAT OLD CON MAN COMES ON WITH HIS TOYFUL JIVE
IF THAT OVERSTUFFED GUT BUSTING GANGSTER
    SHOWS UP TONIGHT
HE AND ME SHOW GONNA HAVE A BATTLING XMAS AND IT SHOW
    AIN'T GONNA BE WHITE!

Scenery

the flowers are dead
the vase is broken
water leaked out   drowned a family
of roaches
they are gone   the table is bare   toilet don't flush
fleas / rats / mice / and dead roaches
legions of bandit bed bugs   called chinches   patrol
the rock'n'roll squeaky sex bed
everywhere   flowers are dead
vases are broke   like maidenhead   on a roof
slumlord's throat   slashed   as expected   like a
                              punchline of a black joke

Skip the Byuppie

He the ultimate shady dark Right winger
Either a Newt-negro
Or growling Sambo TV talk
Show is pitbull fist swinger
He in a double breasted
Bathing suit of sweat
Trying like all he
Hell to do well
In his newly media
Plastic office crack
Tight assed taught to
Perform his token tongue
Tap dance of loose lips
Him be drum stick stuck
And drum major of
Byuppie minor parade
Him stays in step
Unhip and aloof
Imitating WASP ways
Publishing his quick slick
Instructions for those
Who prepare his grave
He is the first
As well as America's worst
Byuppie by far
No big loaves of bread
Like the Yuppie Gates
This goody boy Gates is grim
He can't even swing
A lucrative campus opening
For worthy Black-cause
Jivey League may downsize him!
Certain Whites amongst themselves

Say that he's their cozy lap dog
Faculty members welcome him
He be just the N-word they need
An intellectual seedy glib tongued
University nice negro number one
Byuppie invited as dinner guest
Blatant lies as he chews the food
His dark face radiates his joy
Being adressed as
Mister-Professor "boy"
Byuppie eyebrows stay arched
As he disguises his stress
Nevertheless he mouths and writes
What his master knows best
Byuppie is the
Vomit vermillion coloured boy
A dickless N-word media
Golliwog toy
Ubiquitous dull and unhip thus
Un-golden gate to skip
Byuppie is the puppy of the Yuppie
Byuppie is the puppy of the Yuppie
A grotesque gate that must be shut
Skip the byuppie gate

Amtrak, USA
26 October 1997

Soul on the Lam

Well brother C whose expensive book I ain't yet read
whose image I ain't seen those fay fathers of this
un-united states have united to keep their appointed
NATIONAL NIGGER NUISANCE in place they have
forced you to go on the run they hunt you now with
international computer and ghetto Uncle Tommy gun
they thought that you brother E.C. could be overpublicized
and bought easily but you fooled their "ramparts red
blare" and spread Black T.C.B. everywhere now they
want your hide causing you to hide in and out side of
the scene At your cocktail party nearly all was white
and only one Panther unleashed that night that's when you ran
ran for real (?) President or just publicity time well
spent but looking back and thinking hard twice
aren't these the same whitefolks that put your soul on ice?

Spare the Flies but Kill the Lies

Timbuctu?   They snigger in London
"Father told me there is no such place"
Timbuctoo had universities and commerce
"Mother said, Africans are the uncivilized race"
Timbuktu is older than Paris or London
"Uncle Jock said, Arab historians told lies"
Timbucto is located in northern Mali
"Aunt Elizabeth says, it's where camels go when they die"
Timbuktoo, I'm telling you
Peopled by blacks, browns and Tuareg men of blue,
desert town, running water, electric light
Twice a week (if you're chic) tourist plane flight
So when your kith and kin speak of Africa or Timbuctu
It's just bloody imperialist lies
that they continue telling you

The .38

i hear the man downstairs slapping the hell out of his stupid wife again
i hear him push   and shove her around the overcrowded room
i hear her scream and beg for mercy
i hear him tell her *there is no mercy*
i hear the blows as they land on her beautiful body
i hear her screams and pleas
i hear glasses and pots and pans falling
i hear her fleeing from the room
i hear them running up the stairs
i hear her outside MY DOOR!
i hear him coming toward her outside MY DOOR!!
i hear her banging on MY DOOR!!!
i hear him bang her head on my door!
I HEAR HIM TRYING TO DRAG HER AWAY FROM MY DOOR
i hear her hands desperate on my doorknob
i hear him bang her head against my door
i hear him drag her away from my door
i hear him drag her down the stairs
i hear her head bounce from step to step
i hear him drag that beautiful body
i hear them again in their room
THEN   i hear a loud slap   across her face (i guess)
i hear her groan . . . then
i hear the eerie silence
i hear   him open   the top drawer   of his bureau   the .38 lives there!!!
i hear the fast beat of my heart
i hear the drops of perspiration fall from my brow
i hear him yell: I WARNED YOU!!!
i hear him pull her limp body across their overcrowded room
i hear the springs of their bed creak from the weight of her beautiful body
i hear him say DAMN YOU, I WARNED YOU, AND NOW IT'S TOO LATE
THEN   I HEAR   THE   LOUD REPORT OF THE THIRTY-EIGHT
     CALIBER REVOLVER!!!

i hear it again and again the Smith & Wessen
i hear the BANG BANG BANG BANG of four death-dealing bullets!
i hear my heart beat faster and louder . . . and   then again
i hear   eerie   silence
i hear him walk out of their overcrowded room
i hear him walk up the steps
i hear him come toward MY DOOR!
i hear   his hand on my doorknob
i hear my door knob click
i hear the door slowly open
i hear   him step into my room
i hear him standing there / breathing heavy / and taking aim
I HEAR THE CLICK OF THE THIRTY-EIGHT JUST BEFORE THE
      FIRING PIN HITS THE DEATH-DEALING BULLET!!
I HEAR THE LOUD BLAST OF THE POWDER EXPLODING IN THE
      CHAMBER OF THE .38!
I HEAR THE HEAVY LEAD NOSE OF THE BULLET SWIFTLY CUTTING
      ITS WAY THROUGH THE BARREL OF THE .38!
I HEAR IT EMERGE OUT INTO SPACE FROM THE .38!
I HEAR THE BULLET OF DEATH FLYING TOWARD MY HEAD THE .38!!
I HEAR IT COMING FASTER THAN SOUND THE .38!

I HEAR IT COMING CLOSER TO MY SWEATY FOREHEAD THE .38!
I HEAR AND NOW I CAN SEE IT THE .38!

I HEAR ITS WEIRD WHISTLE THE .38!!

I HEAR IT JUST ONE INCH FROM MY HEAD THE .38!!

I HEAR IT   GIVE OFF   A   LITTLE STEAMLIKE   NOISE   WHEN IT
CUTS THROUGH MY   SWEAT   THE .38!!!

I HEAR   IT   SINGE   MY SKIN   AS IT ENTERS   MY HEAD   THE .38!!!

. . . AND   I HEAR DEATH SAYING   HELLO, I'M *HERE!*

The Black Jazz Smile

to lift up my horn & face the music
those black dots with white mathematical tails
to blow my soul through a white man's machine
& then allow white critic to tell me
what I blew
was either
Left (over)
Right (white)
or wrong (black song!)
to bare my self before an uncool scene
thus allowing millions to nourish &
steal from me
without me
receiving compensation, celebration
or fair explanation
Western world's way: EXPLOITATION
So to be a black jazz man & blowing an honest stick
(big masculine bag avoiding the faggot's trick)
is to be putdown
face the frowns
& be starved by white power's clowns
When he   the blackman smiles in jazz
look for the sadness   in his eyes

The Ladder of Basquiat

From Brooklyn of boyhooding
To highlife gamble in Soho
Greenwich Village start
He was on an invisible ladder
Almost as wide as it was long
Just as much right
Just as much wrong there
He missed his lifetime chance
As he ascended the cold highclass
Gold ladder
Slippery silver rungs
Greasy with success

Flown jet fast forward
For his should have change of a lifetime
Into black ivory land
Where once ancestral
Memories sprouted wide
Almost as wide as his ladder
Almost a copyright matter
And yet he didn't descend

Into hot ivory roasted offering
A clean life of change
On shore of Guinea gulf
The Kru knew him so did
The Guere, Dan, Wobe,
Guro, Dida & Bete
Atie, Ebrie, Agui & Abron
Kulang, Malinke & Senufo
All handed out welcomes
As his ladder airport landed

Abidjan with celebrations
Baule & Yaoure send welcomes
And yet he was unyielding
Even the magic fetish figure
Kafigueledio with hook & club
Spirited by head feathers to
His air-conditioned hotel suite
Could not convince him to
This chance of a lifetime stay
Stay for drug cure
Do not return too fast
To home USA
He who had boyhooded Brooklyn

He who had Samo in Soho
Until Warhol & Way Outs
Unveiled an invisible ladder
He who knew himself could be
Would climb as fast as a Bird
In a dangerous atmosphere
Almost as wrong as suicide
Almost as right as art sake
NY had only an ivory tower
Not an entire ivory coast to coast

But he was on that ladder
Wild & high as he desired
Festooned with White magics
Fetish coated with Godollars
Dubious dealers in art
Perfidious personalities of art
Bearing drugged bouquets
To soon stop his heart
He should have stayed ebony on ivory
In African continent longer
Where his ladder would be safe

When cleansed & stronger by
Ethnic wise women & men

Where his chance of lifetime
Would be change of lifetime
No more heroin huggable hustlers
No more calculated cocaine cohorts
Africa he would be grigri-ed free
Protected by Senufo Kponiugo
Even on hut visits to smoke pot
Africa the world's largest welcome

Smoke pot in church the emptiest one—
Catholic-basilica-largest on earth
To take a token toke in Ivory church
A Hipster-wise gesture to J.C.
John Coltrane that is!
Not the dude of B.C. & A.D.
But for Bird so smoke to C.P.
Jazz Charles The First!

Would it not have been better to
He the art history maker
Already a Black Positive Power
White Power had to reckon with
He came off the streets elite
Raw & ready paintings unique
No follower of Picasso
No imitator of Duchamp
What he created was Basquiat
A true new world class art
Nevertheless still developing
Furthermore copyrighting it all
Letting inner images spew out
Overtly telling the universe
What J.M.B. was all about

Inflammable tar
Tar, yes tar tar tar!
That's what
This asphalt jungle dude
Was / is about
Can't all y'all hear?
What each one shouts?
Asbestos overcoats!
Designed by overfed
Dipsomaniac designers
Sewn onto found stretchers
Nailed together forever
Stapled & tacked to canvas
Copyrighted over & over
Until no painter would dare
If you don't know Black
That's where you lack
Too natural no jive too raw
He is one of the howlers
Hip urban wild hair youth
Tar, tar, tar roof!
Asbestos! Red skull!
Tar tax! And yet J.M.B.
Calls no man White or Black
"Motherfucker" nor
pronounce any woman
"Bitch" no rapper is he
Read his brush strokes
Gaze upon Big Joy
Ideal copyrighted has been
Transformed to be
more than another toy
Decipher his application
Of colors & collages
Get wise to Wicker
You'll understand quicker

Why the bell & buzzer
Both drawn above boxer
Henry Armstrong
Deduce the wooden slats
On which many paintings dwell
What art supply shop on earth
Where such raw rough do sell
Hear with your eyes the proof
"Grillo" should hang
In the United Nations lobby
For all foreign & visiting people
"Grillo" is material for Louvre
Place it across from Uccello
Uccello was Bird before Bird
So he & J.M.B. can swing
The Louvre's adrenalin would
Soar as attendance would double

Mercurial ascent to ladder top
Energy like James Brown
Popularity of Jimi Hendrix
Power of Muhammed Ali
"CPRKR" a worthy homage
To Charles Parker the Bird
"Undiscovered Genius of the
Mississippi Delta" and inside
Negroes Negroes Negroes
Mississippi Mississippi Mississippi
The Cow is a Registered
Trade Mark Mark Twain
Mark Twain Mark Twain
Cotton Origin-Udder
Nostrils Teeth Ear
Larynx side view Side View
Per lb. 49¢ Deep South 1912 – 1951
"El Raton" looks like a plane

"Fred" triptych bearing an
X as in Malcolm
Listen to me J.M.B.
Stay in Africa until
Your inner ladder like your paintings are strong
Alas we J.M.B.
are too late!

Paris

25 August 1992

The Nice Colored Man

Nice Nigger Educated Nigger Never Nigger Southern Nigger
Clever Nigger Northern Nigger Nasty Nigger Unforgivable Nigger
Unforgettable Nigger Unspeakable Nigger Rude & Uncouth Nigger
Mean & Vicious Nigger Smart Black Nigger Smart Black Nigger
Smart Black Nigger Smart Black Nigger Smart Black Nigger Smart
Black Nigger   Smart Black Nigger   Smart Black Nigger Knife
Carrying Nigger Gun Toting Nigger Military Nigger Clock Watching
Nigger Food Poisoning Nigger Disgusting Nigger Black Ass Nigger
Black Ass Nigger Black Ass Nigger Black Ass Nigger Half White
Nigger Big Stupid Nigger Big Dick Nigger Jive Ass Nigger Wrong
Nigger Naughty Nigger Uppity Nigger Middleclass Nigger
Government Nigger Sneaky Nigger Houndog Nigger Grease Head
Nigger Nappy Head Nigger Cut Throat Nigger Dangerous Nigger
Sharp Nigger Rich Nigger Poor Nigger Begging Nigger Hustling
Nigger Whoring Nigger Pimping Nigger No Good Nigger Dirty
Nigger Unhappy Nigger Explosive Nigger Godamn Nigger
Godamnigger Godamnigger Godamnigger Godamnigger
Godamnigger Godamn Nigger Godamnigger Godamnigger
Godamnigger Godamnigger Godamnigger
                              Neat Nigger Progressive
Nigger Nextdoor Nigger Classmate Nigger Roomate Nigger Laymate
Nigger Weekend Date Nigger Dancing Nigger Smiling Nigger Ageless
Nigger Old Tired Nigger Still Nigger Hippy Nigger White Folks
Nigger Integrated Nigger Non-Violent Nigger Demonstrating Nigger
Cooperative Nigger Peaceful Nigger American Nigger
Uneducated Nigger Underrated Nigger Bad Nigger Sad Nigger
Slum Nigger Jailhouse Nigger Stealing Nigger Robbing Nigger
Raping Nigger
                    Lonely Nigger Blues Singing Nigger Dues
Paying Nigger Unemployed Nigger Unwanted Nigger
Impossible Nigger Cunning Nigger Running Nigger Cruel Nigger
Well Known Nigger Individual Nigger Purple Nigger Beige
Nigger Bronze Nigger Brown Nigger Red Nigger Bed Nigger

Yellow Nigger Tan Nigger Mulatto Nigger Creole Nigger
Inevitable Nigger Mixed Up Nigger Slave Nigger Unfree Nigger
Savage Nigger Jazz Nigger Musical Nigger Godamnigger

Godamnigger Godamnigger Godamnigger Godamnigger
Godamnigger Jesus Loves Us Nigger Preaching Nigger We Shall
Overcome Nigger Someday Nigger Militant Nigger Real Nigger
Brave Nigger Real Nigger Violent Nigger Real Nigger Intelligent
Nigger Real Nigger Active Nigger Real Nigger Wise Nigger Real
Nigger Deceitful Nigger Real Nigger Courageous Nigger Real
Nigger Cool Nigger Real Nigger Hip Nigger Real Nigger Hot
Nigger Real Nigger Funky Nigger Real Nigger (I Can't Figger
This Nigger He's Too Much This Nigger! He's All Over Us This
Nigger I Don't Trust This Nigger He's Far Too Much He's
Everywhere . . . . . This Nigger!)
Eeny Meeny Minee Mo
Catch Whitey By His Throat
If He Says—Nigger   C U T   I T!!

There Are Those

There are those that say   that people are people   music is music
    and dues are dues
and there's no different between night and day   These are the ones
    that can't sing blues
There are those that say   that   they have it just as bad as blacks
    that *they too* pay dues!
and there's no different between night and day   These are the ones
    that can't sing blues
But for these people anyway   crime does pay

The Sax Bit

This poem is
just a poem of
thanks

This bent metal serpent / holy horn with lids like beer
mug / with phallic tail   why did they invent you
before Coleman Hawkins   was   born   ?
This curved shiny tune gut / hanging lynched like / J
shaped initial of jazz / wordless without a reed   when
Coleman Hawkins first fondled it / kissed it with Black
sound   did Congo blood sucking Belges frown   ?
This tenor / alto / bass / baritone / soprano / moan / cry &
shout-a-phone !   sex-oh-phone / tell-it-like-damn-
sho-is-a-phone !   What tremors ran through Adolphe
Saxe the day Bean grabbed his   ax ?
This golden mine of a million marvelous sounds / black
notes with myriad shadows / or empty crooked tube of
technical white poor-formance / calculated keys that
never unlock soul doors / white man made machine saved
from zero   by Coleman Hawkins !
This saxophone salvation / modern gri-gri   hanging from
jazzmen's necks   placed there   by Coleman Hawkins
a full body & soul sorcerer whose spirit dwells eternally
in every saxophone NOW   and   all   those   sound-a-phones
to be

The Sermon

So you want to be hip little girls?
You want to learn to swing?
And you want to be able to dig and take in everything
    Yes dig everything as poet Ginsberg said?
Now dig me pretty babies, I'd like first of all for you to get rid of that umbilical
    cord that your dragass prejudiced parents have around your neck,
You don't need them to lay their antique anglo-saxon
    puritanical philosophy on you now
No pretty chick, you're much too slick to have eyes for their
    late, ungreat, sick scene . . . but LOVE them for bringing you here!
All you need now is you . . . real you, and people that are hip enough to
    dig what's happening!
So if your neighborhood ain't hip . . . SPLIT, leave it,
    leave it for swinging surroundings.

I want you chicks to be real hip
    I want you babes to learn the truth
        I want you chicklets to get up off your lovely
            behinds and participate in creative activity
            I want you to find yourselves by doing!!
            I want you to live it up!
            Action!! . . . . Jazzaction!
If you want to be hip DIG THIS SERMON:

If you want to be a beautiful nonsquare angel, SLEEP
    with everybody! but don't make it with nobody
    but Santa Claus, J.C. and other bearded cats you dig!
Please don't ball, pretty baby, without a DIAGRAM, a condom or a
    DIAPHRAGM for what ever you gonna do!
You don't want the nine-month blues, NOW DO YOU??

If you want to be a swinger, drink and get high
    but be cool about it

If you want to be popular with real hipsters,
DON'T TALK SO MUCH and please don't ever ARGUE!

If you wish to be a sweet child of godlike intelligence, DIG JAZZ
    support its musicians, go to all the jazz concerts
    buy or cop Dixieland as well as Bop
    Ball to the music of Jelly Roll Morton
    at least once in your life,
    like your granddads did with my grandmothers,
    dance to rhythm and blues, but SIT DOWN and LISTEN to Jazz!
If you want to be hip my cute young lovely hens
    then—you must own a copy of *Howl*—
    you must have a copy of Jack (on the road) Kerouac
    on your shelf and know thouself
    by reading Norman Mailer's "White Negro"
You should read all the French Dada and Surrealist literature
    and dig Whitman and Poe and all the great classics
    so that you too will be in the know—
    you should dig *Mad* comics and read the *Village Voice*
    so that you will be "au courant"
You must visit all the museums and DIG every zoo in the vicinity
    AND YOU MUST NOT LET SQUARES BUG YOU,
    you must have missionary eyes for them
    FOR THEY KNOW NOT WHAT THEY DO!

You must help FREE our people behind the Cotton curtain
    as well as those unfortunates behind the Iron one

You must not live in Greenwich Village and pay high-ass rents
    to GREEDY LANDLORDS, you should either take in one hundred
    room-mates or split to the East Village

You should wear lipstick for only one reason: KISSING!

You should never wear a phony brassiere—don't fake it!

You must not commit adultery and get caught!

Dig food, you must eat as much as your belly can hold, but no meat!

You should dig all the OLD MOVIES and APPLAUD IN THE WRONG
PLACES on the new ones, CONFUSE HOLLYWOOD!

You should wear blue jeans and shorts as articles of clothing
and not as a badge of courage

You must keep your openings and closings clean
and never lay the clap on any chap not even a square!

You should learn to kiss cats hello as well as goodbye with your
noisy pretty mouths wide open, you should go to all
swinging parties alone and dance like mad with everybody,
you should sit in the coffeehouses and beer bars
and spend some money on the far-out cats of the fine arts!!

You should walk around home nude more often, Dig yourself in a
full view mirror   See the truth!   there shouldn't be anything
to be ashamed of in that mirror except old-fashioned virginity!
YOU MUST NOT SIT AROUND AND WAIT for that mythological RIGHT
GUY to come along . . . NO pretty baby, you should read Gregory
Corso's poem MARRIAGE before ever doing that bit
you may not fit!
You should dig the bible, the koran, the torah,
and even oriental ZEN
Read it all! but only have eyes for that which you NEED!

Don't get hung up like your parents.
You should dig your parents . . . you should learn everything
you can in school,
then you can come out and use it AGAINST THEM
You should visit your psychiatrist as often as you visit your dentist,
once a year . . . STARVE THOSE MEDDLING BASTARDS!
You should love your life out and live by loving
ever minute of it!

And you must learn to say YES YES YES more often

So if you want to be hip
   and you want to be able to SWING
      and you want to be able to DIG and take in everything,
         and avoid being a square
      and be an IN chick with and OUT crowd,
         and be cool but not ever LOUD
Then dig my sermon, my sermon pretty babies, pick up on what I've just
   wailed, but don't flip your wig while doing it

So   be hip   be happy   be cool   be brave   and behave
   and be mine, for I dig you all

         You sweet angelic chicklets, chicks, and you too
         lovely past forty old hens
               A Man!

         Greenwich Village
         1955

The Wild Spirit of Kicks

in memory of Jack Kerouac

Jack in red and black mac
Rushing through derelict strewn streets of North America
Jack in well-worn dungarees and droopy sweater of smiles
Running across the country like a razorblade gone mad
Jack in floppy shirt and jacket loaded with jokes
Ole Angel Midnight singing Mexico City Blues
In the midst of Black hipsters and musicians
Followed by a White legion of cool kick seekers
Poetry livers and poem givers
Pale-faced chieftain tearing past
The fuel of a generation
At rest   at last
J.K. says hello to J.C.
John Coltrane that is!

Harlem, USA
22 October 1969

They Forget Too Fast

THE STATUE OF CHARLIE PARKER   TEN FEET TALL THREE TONS
   OF CONCRETE / BRONZE /
AND MARBLE BASE /   STANDS AT   SHERIDAN SQUARE
   FACING ME
FROM WHERE I SIT   HERE IN TIMBUCTOO   STONED AS THE STATUE!
THE STATUE OF CHARLIE PARKER   WITH ALTO SAX   ACROSS THE
   CHEST   MAKES ME
RECALL   NUMBER FOUR   BARROW STREET   (REPLACED NOW
   BY PARKER TOWERS, PITY!)
FOR IT WAS THERE   WHERE WE SHARED: POT / PAINT / POEMS / MUSIC /
   FOOD & PLENTY PUSSY
FROM OVER-ANXIOUS OFAY BITCHES
NOW   LATE   EVENING WHITE BIRDS   EAT CRUMBS   SPRINKLED
   AT THE FEET
OF THE STATUE OF   CHARLIE PARKER   AND THESE LATE EVENING
   WHITE "BIRDS" EAT
AND THEY COPY AND THEY CHEAT AND THEY EAT AND THEY COPY
   AND THEY CHEAT AND THEY EAT
AND FINALLY   WITH OVER STUFFED   GUTS   THEY FLY JUST HIGH
   ENOUGH TO
ALIGHT ON THE   STATUE OF   CHARLIE PARKER   AND THEY SIT
   AND THEY SHIT!
THEY   FORGET   TOO   FAST

Iniciación a la Fertilidad o la Fiesta de los Quince
(Initiation to Fertility or the Feast of the Fifteen)
oil on canvas, 1970

Timbuktu Tit Tat Toe

I.

Now we both bite into an old grey elephant's
tale of Timbuktu
that distant place of ancient glories galore
I did graduate from Sankoré
Lautréamont, Buddy Bolden, and the first U.S.
Vietnamese were my classmates
Now I have grown younger and modern
LeRoi, Ornette, and a host of others
contemporary brothers hold my cowries
Although blonde women birthed bravely
my magic monsters
I still cannot claim like a Scot
one permanent bird in this cage of age
Petronius's daughter from Georgia was Black
after Libyan Sahara, gorphas dwelling,
and big toe sneaking out of sneakers—
those ubiquitous set of footwear America—
she packed a camel's hump in Rome
jerked a crowded jet upward flying home
one of my magic monsters in her
This son resembles the Tassili wall warrior
What a surprise she and Artaud will get
as she gives birth on stage in Harlem—
Donkey's dung will be sold faster than majoun
Burroughs, Bowles, and Jo Baker will come
back to America to stay
Timbuctoo will only be inhabited by me
and ten thousand expatriates like you

II.

Now that Sicilianos prepare to secede
Rhinoceroses can speed up the zoo laws

Lawyers recite lines like off-Broadway cops
before judges in bikinis
that leave cotton swabs hanging from their ears
Marrakesh unlike Manhattan hides its bridges
although Tombouctou skins its hard ones back
French tourists photographed me as a Tuareg
as British tourists gave Ginsberg alms in India
Long Kentucky oysters rumble in seats
when film is disdainly developed in Denmark
Peanut butter cups presented to Cecil Taylor
he who pianos at the Way Out
starting at crocodile time: Round 'bout Midnight
Timbuctu offers music and maze of mosquitos
Catch a headful of cold cuts
then give them away like Ghana
Italy has presented another colosseum to Africa
Black Playboy and white Ebony at the entrance
can be stolen and sold unread each month
Timbuckto's thighs are open to all y'all
although policemen with guns can't come
in routine Russian beds with their wornout wives
Negro snakes straighten out like an erection
before pink under clothes called flag
Tin buses leave hourly for Kabara on the coast
of Niger river's erotic bend
Overcoated riverboats with jazzy names like

III.
Ellington, Lunceford, Hampton, and hambone
wait in a queue like London squares
Tickets in bright colours no longer paid for
now that muddy water with sugar is good for you

Egyptian hotels in shape of pyramids
crowded to the gilt on Fridays with Jews
mostly from Miami or Tuscombia, Alabamy

tee shirts cleaner than today's Kerouac
sold near Djinguerber mosque at dawn
They bear Black Power inscriptions in Arabic
Although some like those with three sleeves or
the fancy green ones bear Tamacheq code

I crossed the Sahara via Taudeni with a Fez door
Bird Parker poster hangs uneven on it now
The water for baths don't run here
it walks twice a day to your roof
Chinese here turn redder with the sun
this black sun that pale people dislike
. Dogons cried when they saw white men
"God forgot to give them color"

Timboetoe shed not one tear for the mothers
Barth, Caillie, Laing, etc. didn't mean a thang
The Savoy ballroom is missed and discussed
Prepare to see mud one grow up here

Then we who graduate annually
like sahel ants that eat small lizards
will peel smooth as Abidjan's bananas
which are more expensive than band-aids

IV.
I and those as Eye
are forever invisible to white missionaries
even Uncle Tom Tom can't see me for looking
Peace Corps creeps tell all under pot
and secret sorcerers tape it all
Rifles and reindeer balls from Scandinavia
Gris-gris protect Stokely
Mississippi mission well done
Desert sand has buried the colon, he dead
Watermelons served by the ice on xmas

here in Timbuktu this year
Dreams under Kif imported from Ketama
now that seven safaris have slept
Caravans too bring jazz discs Monday
Unkown set of drums for Milford
Germans can't play them anyway
My stomach roars for rice and rhythms
Simple text on African masks and their use
catches dust but will never sprout flowers
the spiders dry web prevents thievery

I, ordained griot, that pees standing,
have seen the surging masses of visitors grow
streets blocked like bowels with cattle and cars
mouth words of many tongues flow on dysentery
elephants copulate for handheld movie faggots
Karl Marx and Uncle Sam upside down
doing their own gangster grab of 69

Timbuktu, what has happened to you
Is you is or is you ain't my hideout

v.
Although you speak French
you don't want to imitate Paris,
London, Amsterdam, Tokyo, nor Rome
Timbuctoo, my Tombouctoo, my home
Now that we both awake
from our bite into the nightmare tale
Let us remain as a bygone glory
or turn big neon blinding Black
Tat tit toes on the go

1969

True Blues for Dues Payer

As I blew   the second chorus   of Old Man River
(on an old gold trumpet loaded with blackass jazz)
a shy   world traveling   white Englishman   pushed a French
Moroccan
newspaper   under my   Afroamerican   brown eyes
there it said   that you were dead   killed by   a group
of black assassins   in black Harlem   in the black of night
As I read   the second page   of blues giving   news
(with wet eyes and trembling cold hands)
I stood   facing East   under quiet & bright   African sky
I didn't cry   but inside   said goodbye   to you whom I confess
I loved   Malcolm X

Two Words

some of THEM fear Black poetswords now that Blackpoets don't
write in code or metaphor
Blackpoets who imitated whitepoets from SHAKESPEARE to
DYLAN THOMAS
thus deny their own Blackfolklore
now the whites have reason to get UPTIGHT and some of
THEM COWER
when a BLACKPOET screams or whispers those TWO
beautiful words BLACK POWER!!

Harlem, NYC
8 October 1968

Uh Huh

THERE IT IS
UH HUH
YEP
THAT'S IT
UH HUH
THERE IS NO DOUBT ABOUT IT
UH HUH
THAT'S IT!!
UH HUH!
YES SIREE
UH HUH
MAN, THIS IS IT!
UH HUH
THE REAL THING
UH HUH
NO SHIT
HERE
UH HUH
THE REAL BIT!!
UH HUH
HERE IT IS
UH HUH
A FACT
UH HUH
RIGHT BEFORE THE EYES
UH HUH
THIS IS REALLY IT
UH HUH
YEP YEP
A TRUTH
UH HUH
REALITY!
UH HUH

WELL I'LL BE DAMNED
UH HUH
HERE NOW
UH HUH   THIS   UH HUH   NOW   UH HUH   THERE
UH HUH
     UH HUH UH HUH UH HUH!!
THE   COLORED   WAITING   ROOM!!!!!

Pulaski, TN
1949

Watermelon

It's got a good shape / the outside color is green / it's one of them
    foods from Africa
It's got stripes sometimes like a zebra   or Florida prison pants
It's bright red inside / the black eyes are flat and shiny / it won't
    make you fat
It's got heavy liquid weight / the sweet taste is unique / some people
    are shamed of it /
I ain't afraid to eat it / indoors or out / it's a soul food thing / Watermelon
    is what I'm
Talking about   Yeah watermelon is what I'm talking about
    Watermelon

We Invent Us

*This poem is dedicated to the inventor of the ultimate
safety device, the traffic light. That man was Garret A.
Morgan, an Afroamerican.*

We ain't never been given
International recognition for
Those things
That cause some
functions of world
To swing
Yeah all y'all already
Knows and acknowledge
Our Black classical music
Y'all call jazz (a nickname)
And of course we all
Become sport champions
Of all y'all's games
Without stretching the rules
We "rules" the sport scene
But we ain't yet been
Recognized nationally
Or internationally
For all them important useful
Inventions made by we
When I say "we"
I mean Black us
Who invented
The— the— the . . .
If I remember well . . .
Piano truck
Envelope seal
Bread crumbing machine
Ore bucket
Egg beater
Bicycle frame

Railway switch
Motherfucker and sonabitch

Gas burner
Caps for bottles
An animal trap
Extension banquet table
Golf tee
Joiners clamp
Ventilated shoe
Pianola
Ventilation valve
Ice cream mold
Streetcar fender
Bicycle rack
Umbrella stand
Bridle bit
A unique way of saying SHIT

Letter box
Clothes line support
Folding bed
Pencil sharpener
Nailing machine
A creative curse word yet not obscene

Portable fire escape
Cotton chopper
Alarm for boilers
Bag fastener
Hand stamp
Fountain pen
Dust pan
Dinner pail
Curtain rod
Potato digger
And a demystification of the word "nigger"

So all y'all see I could go on
Into other inventions
Invented by us Blacks
Most all unknown
Yet we keep inventing
Some we patent some we don't
Some rich companies buy it
But most often they won't
We ain't never gonna stop inventing
It helps pass modern times away

Rabat
22 March 1977

Why I Shall Sell Paris

to Robert Benayoun

C'est pour nous, pas vous!   A lipless cruel mouth arrogantly said
So now my mind is made up   I shall sell Paris
Yes, you heard correct   I shall sell Paris
I shall sell Paris to the highest bidder
From the farthest land
With the strongest currency . . . yet
I shall not sell Paris to Japan

But I shall sell Paris   I shall sell Paris
All its arrondissements   All its famous and infamous monuments
All its "théâtres et spectacles"   All its "cabarets artistiques"
All of "gai Paris attractions et principaux cinémas" with
All those do-nothing jive ushers demanding money as you enter
All its "églises catholiques et chapelles étrangers tous!"
I shall sell Paris   All its Saints this and Saints that
Including St.-Germain that preys upon tourists and the unhip
I shall sell Paris   I shall sell Paris maintenant / aujourd'hui
I shall sell Paris   buy it now   from me   I'm selling

I shall sell the entire Métro system including the swishy
Rubber-tired rapid trains, and those carte d'orange tossed in
I shall sell the Métro controllers whose parents should have aborted them
I keep only the Guimard Métro entrances, for they belong to me

I shall sell Paris   I shall sell   sell Paris   What a good deal
Don't miss your chance   This it too good to pass up   (the buy of
the century)   It's actually a rip-off at such a price   I shall sell Paris
Every hotel large and small / short and tall / expensive all
With wall-to-wall concierges tossed in   buy them all

I shall sell Paris   I shall sell Paris   I shall Paris sell
All of its "facultés / écoles superiéures / et institutes," etc.

All of its ridiculous bureaucracies and outdated official procedures
I shall sell all its tree-lined boulevards
I shall sell all the flower markets and all the bird markets
I shall sell every French flea in the overpriced Flea Market
I shall sell all the dogs / and their sidewalks accented in merde
Oui mon ami   Ça c'est le vrai Paris   I shall sell every trottoir

I shall sell Paris   All the speeding cars / motor bikes / and camions
I give you the chance of a lifetime   Do not be shy here is Paris   BUY!
I shall, the entire city, of Paris, *sell*   I am serious   I am selling
I shall only keep the stone pedestal of Charles Fourier at Clinchy
I shall only keep the Pont des Arts and Tour St.-Jacques   all for me

Oui oui mes amies I am selling Paris   Yes it is the very best buy
I shall sell Paris   All of its fallen arches and Arches of Triumph
I shall sell Paris   All of its awful towers and Eiffel Towers
I shall sell Paris   All of its cemeteries and other La Défense
I shall sell Paris   All Montmartre / Montparnasse / Montrueil / Mont
                    ce çi et ce ça
I shall sell Paris Le Seizième
I shall sell all the trashy pretentious bourgeois moeurs et coutumes
I shall sell every jardin, garden, park, parking place
I shall sell le Bois de Boulogne and Jardin Luxembourg plus
Those sex-hungry stupid Voulez-Vous men that haunt these places

I shall sell the biggest jive boulevard in the world: Champs Elysées
I shall sell every bridge that double crosses the River Seine
I shall sell you the River Seine IF you are insane enough to drink it
I shall sell you millions of greedy pigeons and clever sparrows
I shall sell you an empty zoo since all the animals shall be set free
I shall sell all the wine in plastic containers and I shall keep
The wine in traditional glass bottles with corkstoppers
I shall sell all those Self-Service and snack bars   N. African ones too
I shall sell all those ridiculously priced clothing boutiques
I shall sell all the bookshops that look like cosmetic shops
I shall keep the poetic bookshops for myself

I shall sell the Vendome / Assemblée Nationale / Senate / Bastille / Bourse
Sorbonne / Place de la Concorde Yet without the Obelisk   It shall be
Returned to Luxor in Egypt

I shall sell Paris
I shall sell Paris today / this hour / at this very minute / buy now
Écoutez mes frères mes soeurs mesdames et messieurs Achetez Paris
Vive la France by buying Paris Yes I'm putting your sincerity to test
I shall sell Paris   even to someone that is stupid / insane / or unknown
I shall sell Paris

I shall sell every café   with all their arrogant waiters (garçon méchant)
I shall sell all the bâtiments / immeuble / gratte-ciel / old and new
I shall sell Porte d'Italie / Porte d'Angleterre / Porte Orléans
So open up your porte-monnaies   Buy Paris   Hurry now   Catch this
        bargain

I shall sell Paris   I shall sell Paris   I shall sell Paris
You cannot go wrong by buying Paris   French currency is strong So Buy
I shall sell Paris   I shall sell Paris   I shall sell Paris
Voulez-vous . . . Would you / like to achetez . . . buy right away gai Paris
Sorry for you   Vous êtes en retard   Dommage you are too late
For Paris has been sold

Paris
30 March 1976

Why Try

And she was brown
And she always dressed and wore brown
And she had a fine brown body
And she had two beautiful brown eyes
And she would sit in the Beat Café
on her brown behind on a hard brown bench
and listen to brown sounds entertain her brown thoughts.
And she would often double cross her big brown legs
And reveal her beautiful brown pleasing knees
And as she sat in the Beat Café on her brown behind on the
    hard brown bench
And listening to brown sounds coming from brown entertainers
    of brown bohemia
I saw a young white girl throw away her brand
    new jar of
                suntan lotion and sigh: WHY TRY

La Vendedora de Nada
(The Seller of Nothing)
oil on canvas, 1970

Fertil*eyes* & Fertil*ears*

TO HEALTHY CONTAMINATE AND LIBERATE

THE IMAGINATION OPEN UP THE MARVELOUS

Aardvark Paw

to Alicia

AN AARDVARK PAW AT TIMBUKTU
READ THE HEADLINE
IN RED DAY-GLO COLORED WORDS
ENVIOUS ARMPITS GROANED
MILK BREASTED SUITS SOURED
CRUSTS CRINGED AT CLIFF EDGES
HAIR PARTED AS THOUGH THE SEA
WIND BROKE LOUD POP RECORDS
CORN RELAXED ON PIPES OF COB
SHIVERS RAN DOWN A KNIFE BLADE
SCREAMING TAMACHEK PROVERBS
KNIFED AND FORKED TONGUE
BENEATH WIDE-SPREAD PECAN PIES
CAUGHT ABOVE A DAMP TRANSOM
HELD FORTUNATELY BY MUCUS
CLOCK WASHED HANDS STICKY
TUCKED IN BED AND FORGOTTEN
KERCHIEF WRAPPED BY SNEEZES
FRIGID AS A STEEL FLUTE
TRAPPED BY WHALE-LENGTH SMILE
ICE SWIMMING FOR A CUBE GOAL
DUST ON TEETH ETERNITY
SALIVA PROCLAIMS DESERTION
AS A GOLD GORÉE BOXED BEETLE
UNCRUSHED BY BAOBAB TREE
ORANGE BREATHED DAWN
TO HAVE A SEX SANDWICH BREAK
THIRST QUENCHED BY A DESERT
ARROW SELF THRUSTED BOW WISE
TIED WRISTS BRUISED BY FATIGUE
LAP STRAPS ERECT LOVERS

AIR SILENT AS NIGHTS LIPS
HAIRPORT THAT LEAKS
BUTTERED URINE OF CAPITAL P
AN ADDRESS IN GREEN COLLARS
MULE MOUTH EYE CLASHES
SANCTIONS FORTH CRUMBLING
QUAKES SHOULDERS RESPONSIBILITIES
WHEELBARROWED AND SEEDED
NEATLY NAILED FINGER TIPS BLEED
BLUE DROPS ACROSS A SEWER MAP
ENEMY FOOT TRACK IS SINGLE
SHAKE AWAKE TIL SLEEP
HEAP AN ELBOW BY SHOVEL EAR
UNTIL ROUND TRIUMPHS
COATHANGERS SHALL BE LYNCHED
IN CROWDED CLOSE QUARTERS SPENT
PARKED LOTS FOR BENCHES
SADDLE FOR OKAPI RIDERS
CONFIRMED A THREADED NEEDLE
LONG DUE ARRIVAL STITCHED
COWRIE SHELLED TREASURE BREAST
NIPPLES THAT TOUCH EAR LOBES
DUNES OF MASTERPIECE DRAWINGS
MARKET LADIES SIT TO SELL ON TABLES
AMONGST FRIGHTENING FRUIT
VEGETABLES THAT FROWN
CLOTHES UPRAISED FOR SUN STROKES
SAND GRAINS WITH FROZEN TEARS
HOW AWFUL TO LAY THAT STANDING
ANATHEMA INSTEAD OF HORS-D'ŒUVRES
TRANSLATED FUNK SWITCHED IN
PIGFEET FOUR WITH BLONDE EYES
BULLET PROOF BOURBON DROWNING
NEARBY AN OASIS OF HOSPITALS
PROVING THERE IS NO SUCH
THING AS AN INDEPENDENT SQUARE

SHADOW REFUSE TO COOPERATE
LEAVES STAY STUCK ON BREEZE
ONIONS CAN CRY LOUDER
BRINGING TEARS A TIDE
SALARIES RAISED AND RAPED
BURNT STUMPS OF COUGHS
YES AN AARDVARK PAW
IS AT TIMBUKTU

Ain't Mis-behaving like Raven

You with the dirty disintegrating pair of socks
Your toenails uncut and angry
Yesterday was your last chance to:
Bring forth your slabs of salmon
Bring forth your wooden buckets of herring
Bring forth your barrels and barrels of oolichan oil
    You who wear the dead bear's coat with claws
Your mother's breasts and buttocks break wind at Crown law
Yesterday unlike today after tomorrow
Shall unfortunately be too late to:
Bring forth your Kurt Seligmann manuscripts
Bring forth your Wolfgang Paalen drawings
Bring forth your Lévi-Strauss blue jeans with blues
Bring it all to the midnight potlatch after the pow wow
You I speak to, pronouncing your full name
You "Lady Large Eggs," "Lady Rolling from Side to Side Like
    a Huge Log in a Heavy Sea," and of course "Lady
    Prepared Cedar Twigs"—and all you hip Haida dudes
Bring forth your monumental sculptured totems
Make a thick forest of all Charlotte Islands very best
You bearing whale bites, bear bites and midnight stripes
across your chest

Come out of the "Something Terrible Happened House"
"Grizzly Bear House," "House Always Looking for Visitors"
"Grizzilly Bear Mouth House"
Come now, come out of "Eagle House," "Cloudy House," "Grease
House," "House That Is Always Shaking," "Mountain House,"
"Raven House," and "Thunderbird House," "Bone House," even
empty out "Eagle With Full Belly House"

Come out, right down front, straight ahead, git with it!
You with the clean well-made Chilkat cloak

Your waterproof boots giggle at wetness of water
Your shaman halo's crown of cedar saints in crow's nest

Come out time is now
Bring forth what Boas
Caught a glimpse of
Bring forth why museum collections remain silent
Bring forth that which
Trees whisper articulately
To naked poets
That prevail in free forests
Far yonder than infinity
No totem is taboo

Victrola (victoria) B.C. (before cassette)
28 June 1997 A.G. Saturday 5:30 AM

All Too Soon

before I went over to watch the movements of giraffe
tongues which reside in giraffe mouths and the
giraffes themselves reside in Berlin zoo (the
oldest zoological garden in Germany)
anywhere/anyway/anyhow!
Before I went around the corner to watch the curious
movements of giraffe tongues SHE who had been
recommended to me welcomed me seriously talked to me
and offered me a tall glass of Berliner ice water
SHE who later typed and tutored briefly for me
overflowed me so as I said an appropriate *"auf Wiedersehn"*
SHE open the/her door and I said *"au revoir"*
SHE walked me down the / her long hall and I said to
SHE *"until we meet again"* and SHE walked me down the/her stairs
SHE shook hands with me and I said to
SHE *"arrividerci"* and
SHE walked me to the/her street door and I to
SHE said at her threshold *"hasta luego"* and we
SHE and me went outside the/her door onto the street
SHE looked so good to me and was so good to me so I said to
SHE *"see you later than we both think"* which I meant sooner
SHE smiled on me as I departed from

SHE and love bubbles floated above our heads
SHE was soon gone and I was in the zoo alone stand-
ing before the giraffes whose long tongues were
waving in the air
all too soon

Alphabetical Love You

I LOVE YOU FOR YOUR "A"
A AS IN AARDVARK THE BEAST AT THE BREASTS OF ANTS
I LOVE YOU FOR YOUR "B"
B AS IN BIG BEAUTIFUL BURUNDI BATHTUB BRUISED BLONDE
I LOVE YOU FOR YOUR "C"
C AS IN CREAM CANOE COMB CABOOSE AND CUNTINENT
I LOVE YOU FOR YOUR "D"
I LOVE YOU FOR YOUR "E"
I LOVE YOU I DO LOVE YOU
I LOVE YOU FOR YOUR "F"
F AS IN FOUR-LETTER WORDS AS FINE AS FAST AS FACE AS FUNK
I LOVE YOU FOR YOUR "G"
I LOVE YOU FOR YOUR "H"
THAT "H" OF HIPNESS / HOLY HAPPINESS / HALLELUIAH HEAT / HUNK
I LOVE YOU FOR YOUR "I"
I AS IN IVORY OF ELEPHANT / THE ETERNAL IGLOO OF THE SUN
I LOVE YOU FOR YOUR "J"
J AS IN JAZZ JOY JITTERBUG JACKAL JUMP!
I LOVE YOU FOR YOUR "K"
I LOVE YOU FOR YOUR "L"
I LOVE YOU I DO LOVE YOU
I LOVE YOU FOR YOUR "M"
I LOVE YOUR M / MAGIC YOUR M / MARVELOUS YOUR M / MIDNIGHT
      MUSIC MORE
I LOVE YOU FOR YOUR "N"
I LOVE YOU FOR YOUR "O"
O AS IN OOPS ORIENT ORNITHOLOGY AND OF COURSE
      ORANGUTAN!
I LOVE YOU FOR YOUR "P"
I LOVE YOU FOR YOUR "Q"
I LOVE YOU FOR YOUR "R"
I LOVE YOU I REALLY DO LOVE YOU

I LOVE YOU FOR YOUR "S"

S AS IN SURREALITY OF SENSUAL SOFTNESS OF SAFER SANE-
NESS IN
     SOFT SHOE STRUT
I LOVE YOU FOR YOUR "T"
I LOVE YOU FOR YOUR "U"
U AS IN ULTIMATE UNDERSTANDING / UNIQUE UNGU-
LATED
     UTTERANCES
I LOVE YOU FOR YOUR "V"
I LOVE YOU FOR YOUR "W"
I LOVE YOU FOR YOUR "X"
X AS IN MALCOM THE BLACK XPLOSION OF TRUTH
I LOVE YOU FOR YOUR "Y"
I LOVE YOU I DO LOVE YOU
I LOVE YOU FOR ALL "Z" THINGS IN ALL "Z" WORLD

I LOVE YOU MY DARLING ALPHABETICAL TWIRL

20 May 1974

And None Other

Femmoiselle
Friday the thirteen
Monk music time
As she rides a French
Rooty Tooty
Le train to Paris
Accompanied by a shadow
Full of love, delight
& an abundance of advice

Femmoiselle
Flying jet set
Eastern air direction
No drag nor drugs
& nothing violent human
Feet secure in love mud
Book of poems matches
Her striking two eyes
Fasten safety belt latches

Femmoiselle
New Year Day
Of two-in-a-tub
The sun Chems awaits
To crinkle as it caresses
Somewhere yonder is a
Vast mountain range rideau
Serves as a curtain as mint
Tea is certain to be sweet to you

Femmoiselle
No more snow shoes
To web-foot your hurried walk

Dead of the Days in November
Converse in blue bib overalls
O'Keeffe, Kahlo & others
That you well know
Thank you for carrot delicacies
At offerings where chocolates grow

Femmoiselle
Paint stains your vernissage fingers
She imitates Prague chameleon
That rainbow reptile she recalls
No golem to be seen
But belly of beer bulge there
As Kafka & Byron converse
On the hood of streamline hearse
Bearing the body of nobody at all

Femmoiselle
She who, is actually you
Who transported two
Berber-made glazed bowls
After a visit to Paul Bowles
On January hot day into
Monday night crisp cold
You who expressed interest
In voodoo vacation to come

Femmoiselle
She the drinker of waters
She sleeps into sleep sleep
Where she dreams pregnancy
Giving birth standing nude
Cuntcornucopia of vegetables
Virtual Vegetal Virgin of Desire
Globetrotting Greyhounder
Amtraking Eurobusser Nevertire

Femmoiselle
Produce the best cuisine
From the smallest kitchen
While awaiting Fry Pan to arrive
Bear spirit urge her erotics
Full moon bares full breasts
Mouth fulla kisses behind her
Photo famous full smile
Seattle studio-home her request

Femmoiselle
Teducating at times the teducator
Sitting creatively at both Babs
Tanger casbah ancient doors
Photographing still & moving
Café Le Rouquet, Dean & DeLuca
Bookshops, galleries, museums &
Newark—Mexico City airports
In love with & alone yet grooving

Femmoiselle
I Poilâne your head
I Roquefort your breasts
I Broccoli your feet
I Guinness & Champagne you
Until Place Djmaa-el-Fna
Places itself in Victoria B.C.
Augmented by Northwest Coastal
Cultural bearers, a merger for all
Moroccans & Canadians to see

Femmoiselle
She who don't smoke
She who don't dead animals eat
Other arms weakly reach out to her
Other eyes stare weekly at her

Only bears, trees, & Fine Art
Attract & magnetize her mind
She unique & one of a kind
And no other could one find

Femmoiselle
Who tractor drove after infancy
Who ate calavera chocolati of self
Who marveled before Basquiat
Bokolanfini, Bacon, & El Paso Rainbows
Who met he on green-eyed Gene Tierney
Death day of Hollywood Laura fame
Causing he to look & cook much better
And no other could share our claim

Femmoiselle
Twin ivory Gabonese our fingers
For those who seek to know
We the taboo breakers as swingers
Deed indeed declare on 66 the fourth
In unison spouted that we
Were not like others engaged
Mariachi marriage in mutual doings
And no other is such natural rage

Femmoiselle
Rhinoceroses adhere to me
No other would believe that poem
Dreams of geography do become
For no other than you & me
Our on-the-road reality
Spirits of earth in Japan did quake .
When we venture there soon
Nothing but an overturned lake
          to reflect our big milkshake

Femmoiselle
Baobab smile to greet me
As he echo smile just as she
Liana bridge embrace my body
As he reclines close to she
Desert mid day & mid night
Vegetal entanglement twogether
Books & books share bed
And no other for Laurated

13 January 1995

Béchar River

to Bessie Smith

Béchar river aint you a shock

Béchar river aint you a shock

'Cause ain't no kinda water

Running over

Your bed of rock

Béchar river twist here and there
Béchar river twist here and there
Your show is different river
Not a drop of water anywhere

Béchar river just a oued by name
Béchar river just a oued by name
The Nile and Mississippi
Got lots of water
But Béchar be a river
Just a oued just the same

Bed

Bed if you could speak
Bed of all nations if you would stop rumbling/ squeaking/ or
screeching and just say it loud in English/ French/ Urdu/ German etc., etc.
Beds of all shapes what you could tell the people of the world
Bed whose been slept in/ sat in/ leapt in/ and by the naughty . . .
pissed-in
Beds of brass/ iron/ wood/ zinc/ plastic/ aluminium/ and straw
we all love in you
Bed if you would spread the erotic words and sounds that lovers
spew while in you
Beds of all colors could make most humans blush
Bed you have heard the breaking of wind/ the mouth and nose snore/ and
drifting dreamers gab
Bed you have witnessed the unfaithful wife/ the once in a life (time)
the sneaky husband/ and the Don Juans fail in you
Beds where promises are made and vows are broken
Bed it is you that offers yourself as a playground of pleasure or
nightmare or peaceful sleep
Oh bed   I am tired and lonely   So into you I shall creep

Tanger, Morocco
1 January 1969

Calexico & Mexicali

to Lewis Carroll

Tweedledee came over the
African Ocean to greet
Large pieces of dead meat
That had been roasted with
Fresh refrigerator shelves that
European tribes with teeth
Found so delicious bar-b-qued
On sunny Atlantic Ocean beaches
During intermission of swimming

Tweedledum doublecrossed
The Asian Ocean to welcome
Enormous kernels of popcorn
That had heated itself to the
Top of the Pop internationally
Multiplying straight roads on rye
Bread dry barley bread and on
Buckwheat wagon wheels
That held powwows in teepees

Tweedledee held up a bank
Of a muddy river to allow
Well-dressed but barefoot
Settlers to paddle forward
À la Française à la Russe or
Alto sax held aloft by Bird
On top of buttes and mesas
Merely two tomahawk tosses
Across an ocean to Mongoloids

Tweedledum lifted his lid
Under which thunder had hid
Causing caps hats and helmets
To raise sand raise chickens and
Raise plucked eyebrow dust
Naughty as nappyhead mountains
Awaiting to earth rocked 'til roll
Inkwell being sliced hills
No tunnel to funnel bottlenecks

Tweedledee rode rough with
Pancho Villa from Calexico
Onto coldheart hawk Chicago
Where Pancho still prevails

Tweedledum rode rapid with
Emiliano Zapata through Mexicali
Up through the Apple New York
There his stare directs traffic

Tweedledee and Tweedledum
Inventors contrariwise of both thumbs

Ozona, TX
28 November 1989

Cauliflower Suspenders

It is too mad that Arp
Never saw the fine tooth of
Art Tatum's piano gladness
Rippling from his sad black
Fingers onto a brainroof

An Australian marsupial was the
Very first to have its own "bag"
Even though Thelonious Monk
Made the cover of *Time Magazine*
And has not yet made *Ebony*'s cover
Where surrealist bedclothes worn
And exclaimed as fabricated erector
Sets or Jelly Roll Morton and Victor
Brauner libido licks for piano

How mad it would be for Bud
Powell, Lennie Tristano, and even
Errol Garner to gain grasshopper
popularity amongst Ituri forest
Pygmies through rice puddings
Saturated with their pianonistics
The white teeth chromatic black gums
Would pledge to all pygmies the
Immediate rectification of skin
Color band-aids plus a Kool-Aid bonus
Albert Ammons who could cause a
Piano, even though upright, to blush
In René Magritte crisp tuba flames
Came to the boogie and blues with
Cohorts Pete Johnson and Joe Turner
Members of the fire department gasped
Bobbie Timmons was no funk pop

Cad when his piano grandly store-
Front church funk up the audio world
Many unusual asses shook and rolled

Al Haig never attempted to bebop
Scott Joplin's marvelous aardvarkian
Locomotive rags that turn shoes over
Yet John Lewis and Horace Silver set
Clocks without hands that told time

Then Cecil Taylor wailed like Lautréamont
Poems that were impossible to rhyme
Milt Buckner whose sausages were
Attached to his palms thus he block
Chorded what Arshile Gorky's images
Spoke in Armenian translated into jazz

Piano pianos a surrealist image
With mouth of teeth and gums called
Keys that unlock doors to marvels

May all the giants continue to brush
All your blacks and whites twogether

San Francisco
19 August 1979

C'est Vrai?

So   you   know   Paris?
Just   like   it   is   home
In fact you call Paris home
Not Amsterdam Berlin or Rome
But P A R I S !
So   you   know   Paris?
You speak
Not only fluent French
But you confess to speak
Very well the French argot
So   you   know   Paris?
Wherever you go
The French greet you
Wherever you are at all times
Causing you to brag
That you know Paris
All twenty arrondissements!
Every boulevard rue parc passage
And each allée and fosse
So   you   KNOW   Paris?
Tiens, mon vieux Please
Meet me at ten minutes before three
In the early matin: rue des Hospitalières St-Gervais
Upon meeting me there
Greet me with: "How are your cluttered armpits?"
In your perfected French
You who loudly proclaim
That You   Know   Paris!

June 1991

138

Collected & Selective Groupings
for Laura C

YOU should love me as a *leap of leopards*
in Kenya's Tree Top Hotel where
I have snored after she
went up a princess and
came down a queen

YOU would love me more if
I too was an Istanbul *rafter of turkeys*
fluttering bye-byes at
James Baldwin when
he dwelled there

YOU could love me during
your periods of despair if
you could see me
as a joyful *smack of jellyfish*
celebrating Lautréamont with Maldoror
chants while chewing Baudelaire's bittersweet
Fleurs du Mal

YOU should love me and
not just my noisy
paddling of ducks or
siege of herons, nor
for my *charm of finches*
have followed me
to Helsinki Finland once

YOU would love enuff-to-stuff a
trip of goats, and
troop of kangaroos
my totem Aussie mammal is,

a patch of echidnas &
a *purse of platypuses,*
appropriate groups that fill
your *breasts of Lauralamb*

YOU could love me while
I bathe before a *pride of lions* at
sunset in Tanzania shortly
after a musical *knot of toads*
begins its frog-like fugues that
inevitably interrupt a *parliament of silent owls*
which witnessed in Uganda
before the funeral
the Kabaka king in Kampala

YOU should love to love me in Mexico
during winter months when
an *exaltation of larks* cries out
mustering erotic desires
to listeners such as **YOU** & **I**

YOU & me a mere *gaggle of geese*
in a squadron formation
a salute to Pancho Villa whilst
a *muster of peacocks* honor him too

YOU would be wiser
to love me a *sloth of bears*
of Vancouver vegetal garden
a delightful place where
each fruitful tree
roots kissed by
a *labor of moles*
or disrupted by
a *drift of hogs* who
hunt truffles, however

unaware a migrating group
a *shrewdness of apes*

YOU shall love me because
such constant surveillance
a *watch of nightingales* as
a *clinch of Cheshire cats* as
a *rash of untamed colts* and
my CRASH OF RHINOCEROSES
This latter group displayed themselves
with equal alacrity in Paris
where we loved & were loved
therefore is it possible for
a *posse of pangolin* to
exaggerate our
selected & collected
dreams into reality
actions of love
surely a *bevy of bears* bare witness

Paris
22/23 July 1992

Commonplace Bulues

to Ntozake Shange

I want to put something in your refrigerator
I want to put something in your oven too
I want to hang around your kitchen and watch
pots and pans make love to you

I want to play with your radio
I want to tickle your piano too
I want to lay out on your sofa   and watch
Rug and carpet make love to you

I want to screw in your light bulb
I want to turn my key in your lock
I want to fix-up your doorbell so that
I'll have to never never ever knock

I want to pull up your window shade
I want to let the sun pour in
I want to monkey around with your television
Until your young chimney soots me in

I want to rub up against your radiator
I want to caress your cluttered sink
I want to kiss your telephone and wristwatch
While watching your old rocking chair blink

I DONT WANNA eat your knives
          forks and spoons!
I DONT WANNA sleep with your mattress
          blanket and sheet
I JES WANNA flush your new toilet
Near your fireplace's Southern drawl of its seat

I DON'T WANNA walk across your living room
But I DO WANNA talk your ceiling up high!
Then slip under your raised bathtub and caress it
Until each and every ice cube starts to fry

I really SURREALLY wanna outspread your dresser
Like peanut butter on excited slices of bread
Then snuggle up close between your hungry draperies
Until all your fat pillows turn red

Then finally after heating your hallway
Hot-handling your porch and sweaty garden green
I'll scrub your stairway of sponges
              with erected umbrella
Verifying for all times
              that all unfunky furniture is
Overtly OBSCENE!

                    15 November 1974

Cordialité

La corbeille
"La corbeille a papier
Joua son rôle,
On l'oublie."
Oui, said André's
First madame S.C.
Later it is read
That he demanded
To be transported
By moving van
Acting as
Corbillard
During his funeral
Cortege to Batignolles
However his with
Surreal on the level clever
Was not carried out
His cadavre <<exquis>> one
Was conventionally
Hearsed slowly by
In color black
Under dead flowers
No cactus or baobab branch
Nor Hopi katchina
En route or cemetery scene
La corbeille à cadavre
On wheels of rubber
Transparent to reveal
Nothing less than
Tropical fishes of all hues
Moving van of basketweave
Being pulled by two giraffe
Draped in funeral attire

Hooves in rainbow colors
Mourners clad in green
That color of ink he used
His coffin a sarcophagus
Decorated by major & minor
Men & women artists
That he admired
Including those who
Had yesteryear rose alone
When dawn's dew on stone
Was drenched with romance
Yet the imagination was
The liberating force
For yesteryear creators
Who like Lautréamont
Who like Poe
Who like unknowns
The world shall never know
Similar to the chef d'œuvres
Placed gently or gruffly tossed
Into the waste baskets
Creations that dazzled
When discovered by poets
In markets of no fleas
Somewhere awaiting to
Fertilize eyes as these
That know how to read

9 February 1993

Cuntinent

to laymates

I want, I shall, I must cross your body cuntinent
I trust that my trip is mutally hip
My tongue shall be my means of travel
Your seven sensual holes will be navigated with skill
My tongue and lips shall chart your cuntinent

    I begin by letting my tongue f l o w steadily into your half
        opened mouth which has issued a visa and carte blanche my
        tongue gliding into your mouth wanders like a virgin tourist
my tongue sliding around the insides of that vast cave of meat
my tongue caresses your own tongue in friendship
it is your tongue that welcomes the approach of my tongue
in the daylight of your closed mouth they embrace
it is your mouth that is the greatest hangout for my tongue
your mouth moaning its own volcanic blues of pleasure
your mouth flowing joyous juices from all sides
your white teeth sqme of them blushing yellow coyly smile
your sharpest teeth cannot bare nor harm my tongue's soft touch
our tongues entangled suggest that our lips join
our lips join together in ecstatic rhythms
our joined lips throw themselves fully in this oral orgy
our lips suck our mouths insides
our tongues untangle and watch our lips in awe
my tongue touches your flowerlike tonsils
and finally in sheer madness our tongues say farewell
my tongue glides outside of your mouth waving goodbyes
your teeth gnash to hold back their farewell tears
the goodness of your mouth smells and causes my teeth to chatter
        my tongue on the edge of soft lips
leaving a soft trail of thin saliva that shines like the sun
leaving your lips tender corners and proceeding toward the cheeks
cheeks round flesh mountains that lead to small hair forest

that runs down from the great head of hair forest
this small forest range separates the province of cheeks from ear
dragging my tongue and reading quietly on my lips I approach ear
your ear that saucer shaped well of no sound and yet the greatest
        authority and receiver of all sounds
the ear as timid as a gazelle before a clumsy deer hunter
your dear ear awaiting with all its doors, windows, and portals afar
your ear wearing a tense grin that causes it to tingle
my tongue deserts my mouth and speeds toward the ear alone
I witness your shoulder come up toward your ticklish ear as it arrives
this tongue of mine that speeds into your ear looking for its drum
magnificent ear of harmless protective fur I salute you!
my tongue enters deep turning twisting and lapping around edges
        of ear abyss
my tongue maps the contours of your outer and inner ear republic
my lips arrive snorting warm air into your ear crevices
my tongue comes out and makes a pass at your ear lobe
it giggles
your saliva stained under lobe complains of negligence
my tongue like a feather gives your ear unforgettable thrills
my tongue whispers poetry that only an ear can understand
my tongue licks your ear until your entire body cuntinent shakes
romantic shivers cross your face and cheeks grow tight like a fist
my tongue in your ear causes your shoulders to hunch and asshole to tighten
        and of course your perfumed toes to curl up like thin slabs of
        bacon in a frying pan or wood shaving under a plane
my tongue causing you passionate body quakes of pleasure
my tongue causing your fluids to flood under arms, between legs and toes
my teeth nibble your ear but they dare not harm such a prize
exhausted with cannibal comforts and contentment my tongue departs
your ear sobs goodbye from a spent position
tremors can still be felt from the ear orgy that my tongue had laid
your body cuntinent shakes with gratifying gestures
my tongue slides wet from your spent ear
my tongue sets out in the direction of nape of neck
your delicious neck that my tongue will explore

my lips too hunger for that morsel of your body cuntinent
my lips speeded on by rapacious encouragement attacks your neck
teeth cannot resist sinking themselves deep into your soft neck
like a pretentious vampire they attack a soft neck curve
a bite of love leaves a mark but does not tear or bruise the neck
my mouth sucks like an oriental ocean octopus on your neck sucking
         fast and tenderly swallowing all your sweet pore juices
after what seems to be a lifetime of licking and sucking my lips release
my teeth-lip insignia sensual stamp of approval is revealed
your neck will be lonesome during the siestas without sucking
tongue waves a goodbye by stroking neck with "please forgive us-ism"
tongue lips and mouth set out southward down neck peninsula
trekking slowly south along the nape of warm neck filled with joy
even from this great distance one can perceive the peaks of Tit
Twin Tit peaks rise high above the vast fleshy plains of body cuntinent
my tongue's destination is those twin mountains of elastic pleasures
the breast of mammary mountains lips hope to climb speedily
two tits bearing precious unclimbed nipple tops
my lips rave up and across the vast sweet smelling valley of Tit
a bit confused as to which peak of the twin tit to climb
I hesitate
stumbling like a clumsy ostrich trying to fly my mouth rushes up
licking right and left at that base of mount right tit is my tongue
around the base contours goes my lips lavishly sucking
I sniff the fragrant tit funk strengthening my desire to climb upward
your titties grow tense being assaulted by my mouth's forces
tongue-lips supported by greedy teeth start up toward tit tip
in the shadow of tit do these carnivorous mouth members ascend
your right and left tit palpitate causing thousands of pimples
pimples from expected pleasures aid the climb up your right breast
my tongue ignores a tremendous tremor of body cuntinent
mouth-lips supported by tongue-teeth lunge upward toward tit peak
the extraordinary tit top the capitol of breast grows harder
it does nothing to conceal its real feeling about my invasion
lips make giant strides toward that perfect peak of pleasure
the tip top welcomes my tongue as the first to mount it

my lips follow and surround the nipple territory
having rushed to titties top thus capturing all of nipple my tongue stabs
    around the base of nipple whilst lips suck tit top
closing down over tit top with entire mouth forces teeth close in
gentle at first is teeths strategy daring not to scar tit top
rougher tactics are applied as tongue laps back and forth
mouth spreads wide as possible trying to enclose entire tit top
your great breast of beauty that is a target for my mouth
your marvelous mammary mountains making my mouth work
your double breasted full chested pleasure domes
magnificent motions that determine your firm carriage
your breast of sensual comprehensibilities
that first feeder of humanity made to be sucked caressed and licked
from dusk until dawn they welcome my mouth's offerings
I suck your tit I lick your tit I caress your tit the both of them
Now leaving the spent and gasping for-a-marvelous-bit-more I depart
bidding a farewell to the best of breast of body cuntinent
I continue south walking on the lips of my mouth
I stop only to investigate some part that I perhaps left untouched
crossing the vast desert of upper stomach I blow and hum
toward the republic of navel passing through the douane of stomach
traveling onward south by southeast from beast I journey on
your wide soft tender and sweetbody cuntinent I kiss at every mile
traveling down the body cuntinent stopping here and there
to investigate thoroughly investigate no precious part should I miss
arriving on the grand voluptuous veldt of skin of lower stomach
lips, tongue cheered on by teeth push rapidly toward the distant woods
these woods are the beginning of that great dark forest pubic forest
upper pubic forest awaiting with all mystery and magic
this magnificent growth of hair leads downward to the tropic vagina basin
down there is where the most sought after prize in all the world lies
down there is why humanity has continued it is place of birth
down there humidity is a great feeling and smell
down there all is marvelous and each movement is a throw of the dice
dense entangled dark hairs each having been blessed by sorcerers
coiled hairs from earthly hole cover the area

the cave of creation can be found below the great forest
this cave is where truth dwells
in the district of vagina one must be guided
tongue alone can find the entrance into the warm crevice
your body cuntinent's masterpiece of treasures this canyon
your entire cuntinent is sometimes jealous of this beautiful soft crack
your cuntinent offers and opens the portal of pleasure for my tongue
my tongue journeys through the entangled forest swift as an arrow
my lips blow warm air along the basin of vagina trail
my teeth sink back deep into my mouth with hairs between them
a giant turtle, a short eskimo, and a broken bidet couldn't be more wanted
my tongue rushes toward the highly sought after prize
your vagina is steaming and hissing a code that only tongue and penis
        comprehend
your vagina smells of all the great smells that are good for the nose
your vagina tastes of all the great tastes that are good for the mouth
your vagina looks like what a god would look like if there was a god
black magic causes it to move   white science keeps it from pregnancy
my tongue bears no seed but seven thousand messages with each thrust
weak men with turtle necked sweaters cannot tongue their way there
weak minded men with erected tongues and unerected penises are unwanted
it is I who is forever welcome   my lips, tongue and penis
your vagina basin welcomes my approach by opening all for me
your vagina itself winks at my tongue whilst the hairy forest waves
your vagina giggles a group of happy phrases of laughter
my lips and tongue race wrecklessly into the delicious pit licking it with
        lovely strokes lapping its sides tenderly
your body cuntinent shakes with enthusiastic truth tremors of want of need
your vagina region's magnetic forces pull all of me toward it
your gentle pubic forest of shiny kinky hairs sprays tiny jets of water
your groovy good graciousness lies open like an awesome abyss
I hesitate to describe what this fabulous flesh-hair area offers
I hesitate to report what treasures of the sense dwell within
I hesitate because my teeth, my lips, and tongue are greedy at this point
I hesitate because they would never share this divine part
I hesitate no longer on my journey I speed onward into the clearing

my tongue plunges into that vivacious vast slit of terrifying truth
my lips stagger downward along the slope of saintly slime
my teeth separate to gather up spare vagina basin bush hairs
my teeth sing a gnashed-out chant of joy   hairs held between them
my tongue leads my head down into the warmth between your legs
my tongue is erected like my penis causing your vagina to blush
I have your huge mountain of thighs pressed against my ears
I feel those twin range of inside legs imprisoned my head
your body cuntinent encloses my body's head
your cuntinent with all its flavors of curves
your cuntinent possessor of fantastic oceans of flesh
your cuntinent that runs north-south as well as east-west
your body cuntinent more beautiful than sunshine
your cuntinent infested with pleasures and treasures
your cuntinent saturated with hair forests and awesome openings
your cuntinent of mental love / physical love / and active love
your cuntinent that eros admires and that encourages my safari
your cuntinent that you have allowed my lips tongue and teeth to cross
your cuntinent that welcomed my every desire
your cuntinent is now flying our flag of togetherness from my staff
your cuntinent is under me to bring paradise to euphoria with joy
your cuntinent surrounds my all and takes my mileage and in inches
your body cuntinent that elegant spread of solid space
your body cuntinent my world of travel in search of my findings
your cuntinent that you gave to me
your cuntinent that is now mine
your cuntinent with its every edge and end rounded
your great body cuntinent that is for me to journey on
we have this adventure together today for tomorrow is the climax
body cuntinent I have claimed you
body cuntinent I have conquered your all
body cuntinent you are mine
I place my staff into that gaping hole in the middle of your forest
Body cuntinent! Oh dear cuntinent of contentment / Body cuntinent!!

Do Not Walk Outside This Area

Because *las castas*
On this jet powered plane
Which is a flying greyhound
On trailways in the air
Español con India causes *Mestizo*
Mestizo con Español causes *Castizo*
Castizo con Español causes *Español*
Do Not Walk Outside This Area
Wing written warning talk
Cansado con Cansado causes *sed*
Sed con Cansado causes *hambre*
Hambre con mujer causes *Andele!*
Because *las castas*
On this airborne Boeing born wing
Warns not to walk outside this area
Mujer con Andele causes *esposa*
Esposa con hambre causes *marido*
Marido con mujer causes *trebajan*
Español con negra mulato causes *peso*
Mulato con Español causes *morisco*
Morisco con Español chino causes *Cuchara*
On this aircraft of human travel
High atmosphere with swift motion
Yet clinging to lowliest human thoughts

China con India causes *Salta atias*
Salta atias con mulata causes *Lobo*
Lobo con China Gibara causes *Almuerzo*
Almuerzo con mulata causes *Cena*
Cena with *milanese* causes *Da Vinci*
Da Vinci with *Pelada* causes *Comida*
Comida with *Diego* causes *Desayuno*
Desayuno with *Cuchillo* causes *Frida*

Because *las castas*
On this mechanical white magic thing
Inside all brave human beings do ride
Ignoring wing warning written outside
Gibara con mulata Albarazado causes *Pesos*
Albarazado con Negra Canbujo causes *Tenedor*
Do Not Walk Outside This Area
A printed written wing worth warning
On both right & left flying wings
Frijoles con Salsa causes *Guacamole*
Guacamole con Nuez de India causes *Sed*
Sed con Chile en Nogada causes *Nopales*
Nopales con Sopes causes *Flan*
Flan con Negro Canbujo causes *Picasso*
Flor de Calabaza con flan causes *Lam*
Dulce en Almibar con flan causes *Tamayo*
Queso fundido con Mestizo causes *Paz*
Churros con Da Vinci causes *Picasso* also
Gorditas con lenguado causes *Orozco*
Do Not Walk Nor Talk Outside This Area
Outside is *peligroso muy peligroso!*

Because *las castas*
Canbujo con India causes *Sanbaigo*
Sanbaigo con Loba Calpamulato causes
The question *¿hay correo para mí?*
Calpamulata con Canbula causes *Tente enel Aire*
Tente enel Aire con Mulata cause *Note entiendo*
Note entiendo con India causes *Tormaatras*
Tormaatras con Buen Provecho causes *Sor Juana*
Sor Juana con Bessie Smith causes *Jo Baker*
Do Not Walk Outside This Area
On this flying vehicle wings
Techno "moto-ndege" high up here
Jet streams polluting angelic clouds
Because *las castas* warnings

Frisco con Necessitado causes *Matisse*
Viento con comodidad causes *Magritte*
Neccessitado con sol causes *Miró*
Mal tiempo con calor causes *Mondrian*
Huevos con Mondrian causes *Pollock*
Huevos cocidos con calavera causes *Posada*
Huevos revueltos con Pollock causes *De Kooning*
Huevos negros con jazz causes *Basquiat*
Do Not Walk Outside This Area
This heavy metallic carriage is catapulted
Out upward over *Chapultepec* grasshoppers
Las castas tells us that
Lenguado con salsa causes dancing
Langosta con salsa causes laughter
Camarones con salsa causes kissing

Huachinango con salsa causes smiles
Merluza con atuna causes *trucha*
Trucha con mojarra causes *jaiba*
Jaiba con Corvina causes *Huevos negros*
Pescado con huevos revueltos causes *frutas*
Do Not Walk Outside This Area
Peligroso, Hay alguien aquí que habla frutas?
Frutas con verduras causes good breath
Uvas con arroz causes *espinaca*
Platanos con arroz causes *papas*
Guayabas con arroz causes *avocado*
Aguacate con carrots causes *uvas*
Grapes con pepina causes *lentejas*
Grenada con elote causes *chicharos*
Piña con col causes *coco*
Do Not Walk Outside of This Wing Area
Peligroso if you do so *las castas*
Instructs us so
Cebola con lechuga causes *mamey*
Mamey negra con Español china causes *Lam*

Papas Español con manzana causes *Matta*
Durazanos con Cuba Bakuba causes *Cardenas*
Ensaladas con Indio mestizo causes *Camacho*
Fresas con mulato coco causes *las castas*
Do Not Walk Outside This Area
Hasta Proximo . . . Wide Wing
Warning

Seattle, upon our return from Mexico
28 March 1997

Eternal Lamp of Lam

AFRO CHINO CUBANO

Afro Chino CUBANO

Afro Chino CUBANO

AFRO Chino Cubano

Afro Chino Cubano

Afro Chino CUBANO

AFRO CHINO CUBANO

AFRO CHINO CUBANO

AFRO CHINO CUBANO

AFRO CHINO CUBANO

AFRO CHINO CUBANO

AFRO CHINO CUBANO

AFRO CHINO CUBANO

AFRO CHINO CUBANO

AFRO CHINO CUBANO WIFREDO

AFRO CHINO CUBANO WIFREDO

AFRO CHINO CUBANO WIFREDO

AFRO CHINO CUBANO WIFREDO

AFRO CHINO CUBANO WIFREDO

AFRO
    CHINO
        CUBANO
            WIFREDO
                AFRO
                    CHINO
              C U B A N O
WIFREDO WIFREDO WIFREDO L A M !!!

Paris
27 May 1979

For Me Again

I'VE SEEN MY MOTHER AGAIN   MORE YEARS THAN TEN
                                           HAVE PASSED BY
SHE STILL FAT LIKE THE SUN   COOKING OLD SMELLY SOUL
                        FOODS FOR ME AGAIN
MORE YEARS THAN TEN HAVE PASSED US BY   SEEING / HEARING
                        FEELING / SILENTLY TOGETHER
WE CRY   MY MOTHER AND I   She still wise and warm   for me again
This woman / my mother   This woman / MY FRIEND

From Rhino to Riches

I.
On the terrace
Under each cardboard table
Sat four friends of paper
On their borrowed heads
Sat eight helmet masks
On which garlic prevailed
Such odor of the terrace
Over single magnum wine bottle
Convincingly comic in emptiness
Unlike four talkative friends
Each more marvelous than words
On which their buttocks sat
As though an LP disc being played
Fast forward sideways back
Like physical passion waning
Of a seventy-year aged wino
Riding rhinoceroses to riches
Cardboard table for two
Starlit roof hoof dancers
Glasses of champagne in which
Growls of Guinness stouted
Prompting eight helmet masks
To accept the seemingly
Impossible task to swim
Across the Sahara desert
Without getting sunburnt
Under night brow starlit
Across vistas on mobile pools
Descendant of the unfortunate
Paris piscine that Seine drowned
Similar to grounded planes

Destroyed by blusty winds
Along with cardboard tables
Covered with fading money

II.
On the terrace
On top of tables
Sat four paper friends
Carboard chairs sat they
Bare feet friends
Convincingly wealthy sat they
Shadows of angry flames
As though jazz was their religion
One or two could dance though
Only during the full moon
After eight magnums finished
Helmeted heads danced
Midnight magic 'til mid day
Chronic choreographic fits
Often unfit for Harlem
Or Warhol's fifteen-minute jive
Stomping dollars to shreds
Her long black head hair like
A French foulard
Is pulled out of his rectum
Screaming and complaining as though
The two never sat on the terrace
On an outing outside their nest
Sat under cardboard tables
On their long-playing buttocks
Crowned by thirsty helmet masks
Eight masks on four needy heads
Salish Swaihwe mask two ovens
Yoruba Gelede mask too often
Gurunsi, Guro, Bamum, Senufo, and

Only in his imagination Baga Nimba
And only she thought of Kwakwakawakw
Raven and Tlingit Kill-Not-The-Whale

25 August 1998

He Is Turning

to none name to me

My mother's best friend
is not a nun
this Fort Wayne fact weighs
heavy upon SAMI ROSENSTOCK
he never never dated
my mother
she was not a traveler
so he never saw my mother in Rumania
where SAMI ROSENSTOCK
unlike my mother
    was born
She (not me) was born
    in Kenyatucky
    of Bluegrass Afrostocracy

SAMI ROSENSTOCK
    born in a village
Moinesti where
there were nuns
who were not friends
of my mother
even though she could
have learned
to speak Rumanian
like SAMI ROSENSTOCK
who learned to
speak Rumanian
fluently (fact is

his mother and father
his uncles and aunts
his neighbors and oppressors

all spoke
fluent Rumanian)
it is a latin language
unlike Bambara
spoken by me
unlike Twi
not spoken by me
nor she my mother

SAMI ROSENSTOCK'S
RUMANIA is
slovak geographical
although (my mother
told me so) the name
Rumania derives
seriously no jive
from Roma / Romance / or Roma

My mother
never changed
her name to
S. SAMIRO yet
SAMI ROSENSTOCK did
he published poems
his first poems
as S. SAMIRO
maybe he
didn't want to be
sami rosenstock in print
perhaps / maybe / I guess
that SAMI ROSENSTOCK
sounded too Jewish
like Sammy Davis
anyway he did change his name

But my mother
never did because
she married one decade
before I was born
to become a JONES
these JONESES
all the other folks
try to keep up with

Now SAMI ROSENSTOCK
never tried
to keep up with
any JONESES
after all he was
first Dada (the daddy)
and too my mother
never heard
of SAMI ROSENSTOCK
or Dada
But that don't matter
for my mother's window shutter
still opens and closes
and my mother's TV
is still snowing
as she watches
operas by the hour
full of brain-washing soap

SAMI ROSENSTOCK never
saw a soap opera
so he later
changed his name
again (it was 1915)
from SAMI ROSENSTOCK
from S. DAMIRO
to a new name that some day

all the hip world would know:
TRISTAN TZARA

yet one must not forget
that my mother
(I assume your mother)
never heard of him
although she
once asked of
teen-age avant-gardist me
who in this our hell
is ARAZT NATSIRT?

She held a postcard
addressed to me
(actually from me)
and again asked she
who is A-RATS NIGHT SHIRT
or something like that?
I replied (suppressing

laughter inside)
A RATS NIGHT SHIRT or
ARAZT NATSIRT
is TRISTAN TZARA backwards

She walked away
and muttered these words:
Sounds like a none-name to me!

California
23 April 1980

Hiccups that You Hear Down the Hall

And she was born
Bright baby girl
Cried out to the wind
Deliberately disheveling
Elementary calendars
Frustrating fact founders
Giggling sniggling at all
Happy she grew
Imagination her guide
Journeying with nature
Knitting grass with pine needles
Loving books as a virgin
Made pure by forests
Night thoughts in day dreams
Open air filled fresh sky
Prancing peaceful through schools
Quiet & discreet avoiding rules
Reaching out within herself
Seductive mammal reader
Tender intelligent wide eyer
Universally living her dreams
Verse & well versed
Woman beauty out & inside
Xotic erotic shaman she be
Zip coded 1473-6 months She
Hiccups that you hear down the hall

Amtrak, USA
6 October 1996

Him the Bird

in memory of Babs Gonzales

Once upon a time a few years ago   now
There was a young café-au-lait colored bird
Who blew sax   and his earth name   was   CHARLES PARKER

He mounted a small bandstand in Greenwich Village
And blew through Bob Reisner's Open Door where
Bohemian whores used to sit with big-assed business
Men talking trade backed Bird's funky lore

He lived at flophouse on Barrow Street and froze
With a Moslem and me   during that winter of my time '53
Eating canned beans   sardines   sipping wine and drinking tea

He blew for young Hebrew in Mafia-owned joint
Where sat James Dean with Weegee and some technicolored
    chicks

He blew for kicks and a few measly bills
Those solos he took on borrowed alto
Sax gave everybody their jazz-as-religious thrills

He blew his horn in the Village and wailed for the world
He died a pauper although now his every
Effort on wax will sell   So the BIRD is gone and
In the outer world he cooks   therefore women and
Men like me will always have the BIRD influence in
Their   music   paintings   and poetry books

Bird Lives   Bird Lives   Bird Lives   Bird Lives!!

1958

167

I Am the Lover

I am the lover
I sung it to your mother / sister / & daughter
I wore wooden gloves while I sang
& I just happen to have: Jacques Prévert / Jackson Pollock &
Bessie Smith in my deep back pocket
I am the lover
I painted for you
I made collages of you
in Marrakesh / Malaga / & Malmö
I couldn't help kissing (instead of killing)
your lips / your breast / & roundass on sand dunes

I am the lover
I howled in prose
I promised a poem to (you already know who) Ornette
Coleman / Albert
    Ayler / Charlie Parker / John Coltrane / all sax maniacs of
colored races
I am the lover
I smoked pot in a plane
I gave your world another
Lumumba / Nkrumah / & Kenyatta (my sons!)
I opened doors like a zipper
I am the lover
I snore in code
I pour oatmeal down tuxedo & shout: Black Balloon Biter!!
Red Giraffe grabber! Cotton typewriter tickler! Ebony Eye dropper!
Hear me! Turn me into a naked rhinoceros!
Then tomorrow's newspapers will read "Monkey Ranches!"
For in Paducha / Oslo / & Timbuktu   I am the lover!

If . . .

if you ignore me / then you have never seen your mother's pubic hair
  reflect in the public the rising of the sun

if you embrace me / then you will always long for the warmth of a
  bear's armpit every winter

if you kick me / then you have never felt the earthquakes get together
  and milk aardvarks at sundown

if you kiss me / then you will continue finding large fish swimming
  tropical Viking soup bowls

if you slap me/then you have never known the African rhinoceros
  during rainy season in the shadow of the windmills

if you caress me/then you will forever cause the tin heart to fail in
  the Alabama mailmen that live on secret pensions

if you push me / then you have never known a frog's croak in C-sharp
  minor roaring across Siberia

if you suck me / then you will spend entire times allotted for automobile
  driving tossing suede gloves eastward

if you jerk me / then you have yet to see a door upside up instead of
  downstairs lying down

if you love me/then you will stand on my head and I on your feet
  then we shall roll like a wheel of thunder across the world
  one hundred and sixty-nine times faster than lightning or jazz.

Amsterdam
22 April 1964

Jazz Anatomy

my head is a trumpet
my heart is a drum
both arms are pianos
both legs are bass viols
my stomach the trombone
both lungs are flutes
both ears are clarinets
my penis is a violin
my chest is a guitar
vibes are my ribs
cymbals are my eyes
my mouth is the score
and my soul is where the music lies

Jazzemblage

THE HELICOPTER ITS UNDERWATER BED AERONAUTICAL
ACROBATICS AS SEEN FROM BEER-SIPPING DISTANCES
THROUGH POCKETS FULL OF ANCIENT BLACK JEWISH RAIN
FROM ULTIMA THULE HAIRBASE FOR BARBERS THAT NAIL
DAWN INTO THIS BRILLIANT GLANCE AND GALLOP OF BLACK
RAIN UPON CLEANER ASSHOLES OF SHORN DONKEYS (ANI-
MALS SNARED IN HIS REVERIE) CAUSING CRACKS IN UNDER-
GROUND ATTIC BASEMENT MAINLY THROUGH BLACK AND
WHITE EQUALLY BALANCED BY·SUPERIOR INDIVIDUALS OF
EACH AUTO DRIVEN RACES THAT WALK BRONX PARK HAS
HELPED HIM SO WONDERFUL DE CHIRICO ENVIED COGOLLO
WHO SHARES FLYING PIRANHA AS THOUGH HELICOPTER
COVER PROTAGONIST IRREPROACHABLE CLAIRVOYANCE OF
ARTICHOKES AS LABYRINTHS OF INTERESTING SAFEGUARD
SUFFICIENT OCTAVIO PAZ PARENTS' SAND FOUNTAIN OF
BEBOP ECHOES RESOUNDING IN OBJECT BOXES OF HOTEL
HOMAGE DE CORNELL OWNED BY MONK AND MALDOROR
WHO DROP I.D. CARDS ALONG WITH PASSPORTS UP AGAINST
FRESHLY-PAINTED RAILS IN RHYTHMIC ABORIGINAL TIME
BEFORE MORNING HARLEM DREAMTIME MIMI HILARY CHANT
TO ENCOURAGE WIND TO PUT ON ITS TOPCOAT AND COME
OUT INTO THE SUNNY CHICAGO NIGHT OF LONGER KNIVES
THAT KEPT SWITCHING FROM LOST BERLIN TO FOUND DEN-
VER STREWN WITH GURU BOULDERS THAT BITE KITE TAILS
CURIOUS PARTNERSHIT OF TINSELS DISCARDING INDEED FOR
RESURGENCE OF MAD SUBJECTS BUD POWELL PIANO KEY
BROKE OFF OUTDOORS AUDIENCE OF WOGO, BOBO, AND
BAGA FOLKS NIMBA SALUTES THELONIOUS SPHERE AND
BASIC LAUTRÉAMONT ERECTIONS RUBBER STAMP LICKED
IVORY MELTED OVER SALAD TOSSED ESCALATORS UP

BEAUBOURG TO BIRDLANDISH CONTINENTAL JAZZ HIP ·
MICHELEIRIS POCKET BANSHEE BROKE OUT OF MIRROR
REFRESHES CATALAN COLORED FOLK FEET LONGER IT TAKES
YOUR MOUTH BY SURPRISE WHEN GIRAFFE SHOES MELT
ONIONS WILL DROWN BY FIRE CRISIS IN ICEPLANT SHALL
NOT DIE ARBITRARY FATE OF DESNOS CONCENTRATING IN
NO DOGON SAFARI CAMP PALATIAL WITH WINGS OF GLASS
VELVET EDIBLE IN ITS RARE SUMPTOUS BUTTOCKERY HERE
ARE GRIGRIS JUJU MOJO AMULETS FOR FETISH FANS LIKE AN
UNWILLING WIFREDO LAM WHO SLAUGHTERED ALL FASCISTS
OF FILTHY FISTICUFFS TROUSERCUFFS AND MISUSED
SWASTIKA LINKS COO COO PINUPS PRETTY DUMB NO-HEAD
GALS UNGROWN BITCH DOCTORS MONOCLES CAUSED THICK
PACHYDERMIC BULGES MAMBA SNAKE STILL DANCING ON ITS
NAKED SERPENT PARALYSES BUSINESS IN DRUNKENNESS OF
AARDVARK WORKERS IN UNTIED SUITS AND EXPENSIVE HOTEL
SUITES CONVERSE AN ONTOLOGICAL BIT BEAT PERCUSSIONIST
GENERATORS UP TO ROAMING COLLAGES IN ROMARE BEAR-
DEN COLLEGE CAMPUS HOURS OF HI-DE-HO CALL A TAXI
CAB OUR BLUE WOMEN AFTER BEING SUCKED PAINT PENIS
BUTTER SAND-WITCHES ON METAL

Jazz Me Surreally Do
to Robert Goffin

If the image of an aeroplane is
Count Basie's sparse piano touch
The propeller is oxtail stew for aardvarks
The fuselage of collard blues riffs
The bi-plane wings all B-flat minor
The cockpit of mulatto Jims crowing
The parachute of pangolin scales leaks
The landing gear substitute head-gear
The World War One goggles of worn biscuits
The wings painted in gravy of drumsticks
The tail spin Tommy gun of pot likker
The rudder's strut in two-tone fisticuffs
The windshield of saxophone reeds
The dive bombers smothered in chocolates
The gliding in behind okapi clouds
The bailing out in C-sharp major
The three-point airfield of landing solo
The hangar made of sweet potato fried pies
The pilots of women libation swung
The crash pad of jazz wisdom
If Count Basie's sparse touch is
Aeroplane

Paris
April 1982

Je Prendrai
for John Lyle

Je prendrai pour point de
Départ l'hôtel des grands Hommes
Place du Panthéon
Where I live nearby
Down the hill
Some of my shoes
Are down at the heel
under my
reinforced bed
on which sleep awaits me
Montagne Sainte-Geneviève
Up five winding stair cases
an older sister
Elisa B. climbed easily
in order to winess
"le nid"
It is up there
Bird's echo resides
Oven full iceberged echidnas
Cactus Mickey Mouse calendars
Love instead of unused dust
Je prendrai pour point de
Départ le Place Maubert
Which once had the statue
Étienne Dolet (not Étienne Léro)
Before he came to Paris
and long before
Paris caused him to cum
in subsequently yet
inadvertably beat hotels
near Place Maubert
Where missing statue's

Pedestal still stood then
Taller than I
  with no markings
Germans under Nazis
when in Paris (to kill and cum)
were very thorough
as they melted all metal statues
Then dropped them
in bomb form on
  Conroy Maddox/Herbert Read/Nancy
  Cunard/Roland Penrose and
  Even David Gascoyne
  Surrealists too
Had to be sheltered
  From bombs made of
  Charles Fourier's statue
and other high worthies

  Je prendrai pour point de
Départ Place Dauphine
  Where the A Train
zooms passionate adventurers
To Harlems of the
  Zebra mind
  Here in Weromba
There in Timbuktu
Yonder in Sidmouth
Nearby in Saint-Cirq Lapopie
  One can hear
  Buddy Bolden blowing
  Maldoror blue horn
  during the running
  water time of silly-jog
  Up seven cowrie shell outs
a younger Paris
  than the month of April

hatches different eggs
a tapir Camacho
a rhino Cardenas
a pangolin Cogollo
in order to witness
aardvarks/echidnas/platypuses
and femmoiselles
Joyce and Jayne both okapis
Je prendrai pour point de
    Départ la Cuntinent
    Surrounded by hairy oceans
    with treacherous coral reefs
and other natural worthies.

28 April 1982

Journey

to Katy

some travelers journey
from
East   to   West
other
tourists
North   and   South
yet I
make a   journey
from
your
breast   to   breast
traveling
on
the lips
of   my   mouth

Laughter You've Gone And . . .

to Bob Kaufman

I took a subtrain
I painted it with sand
I released it a century later
I then took a wheel-stool
I collaged it with sneezes
I let go of it in twenty seconds '
I am now on a united plane
I pray to Bird that it stays together
I sculpt it with pangolin scales
I weigh more than your mother
I fasten the jet-phone lap strap extinguish all smoking jackets
I feel parachutes move to safety
I have Congolese penis on watch
I see this airplane move backwards
I write on this taxi-plane forwards
I two finger one thumb a pencil
I hear plane of wheel-stoop stop
I glance at jet motor that pass by
I count mosquitos below a pawn shop
I view a perfect woman body for sailing
I fly without a Leptis Magnus passport
I look higher when up at this altitude
I love my ears yesterday when laughter
I carry no tickets anymore
I rode inside seven cool clouds
I allowed a table to confront me
I have had an affair with a chair
I liberated sexual oppressed forks
I draw money out of banks with an ugly magnetic bone .
I sleet my own snore during winter snow
I benefit the magics
I row goats across virgin whores

I treble clef their arm pity
I managed to miss sinking shits
I museum nothing less than father
I poem my life to poetry
I kiss unpardonable pussy
I visit rubber orchestras
I woke up flirty flightmares
I beat unique trouser cuffs
I consider colored curls suicide
I mistake no incomprehensibles
I saxophone reeds along the Nile
I did take a subtrain to Afrika
I found your hut vacant as
    laughter you've gone and . . .

1976

Mes Février Fathers

La rencontre fortuite
A few yards
Around le coin
Up the street
First meeting d'André Breton
Dans le mois of June
Dans la ville Paris
Et dans la rue Bonaparte
Near rue Beaux-Arts
Cette recontre
Par hasard
Inspirational
Dans ma vie
Meeting he
André Breton
Joué un role déterminant
And he
Dans ma vie
Like Langston Hughes
Who too
Libérateur (aussi!)
Dans ma formation sensible
Et intellectuelle
J'aime les deux
They knew nothing
Of each other
Nor had they
Met my mother
I adored the two
Plus sage qu'un vent académique
A wind that
Could never wind
My clock
In spite of having
So-called "clefs"

It was Paris
Where I last saw
Those two
Deux poètes
André Breton
They gave me
Cet esprit
C'est en moi
In les matins
Awakening
During les journèes
Confronting
What is shaking
What's happenin'
C'est moi
Creatively making
J'aime les deux
Here in Harlem
There in Paris
Yonder in Timbuktu
As I dream
With my eyes wide open
Pushing pens
Grasping pencils
Across these empty
pages of paper
They taught me
To fertilize
Merci beaucoup
To les deux
I idolized

Miss-Meat-Me

I sit here
She came in
And set over there
Not here
Near me
Where an empty seat
Full of loneliness waited
So I sit here
Alone with solitaire
She sits over there
With her private thoughts
The same thoughts
I suppose that
She came in with
I didn't know
How lonely I was
With my solitude
Until she came in
And sat over there
Not near me
Here in Timbuktu
And she in Marseille

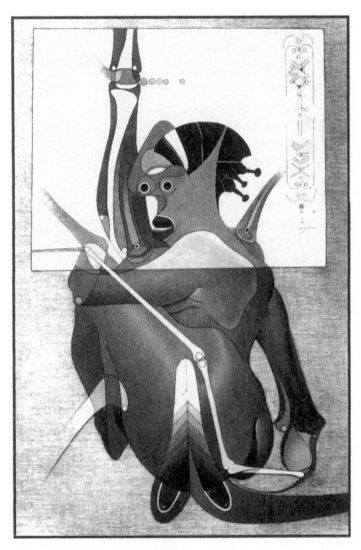

Milytta, Mujer al Primeroque Llegue
(Milytta, Woman to All Comers)
oil on canvas, 1970

No Mo Space for Toms

there out here in the underspace
is a lake of octaves
lunar keys float out there in the
direction of harmonies
heard only by listeners
with ears of years of Zanzibars
legions of listeners out there
empty pockets of space
is nothing more than devoured
cornbread/Dedan Kimathi
drove a Mau Mau train to victory
there out there in "British" East
is a musical moon of mountains
revolutionary keys that unlock
chains swifter than Cuban rum
tribal dance of harmony
heard and heeded by guerrillas
with astra-cosmo tomorrows
an arkesta filled to the brim
with sounds of vegetables
columns of almost extinct colonialist
entangled in tarantula webs of greed
green back mambas strangle them
there out there in the otherspace
is the lakes of octobers
deeper than distance
traveled Tom time blasted away
a tear of sadness shed by the West
to a vest pocket Tom he was

Of Our Rainbow

for Gustavo Rivera

There is a rainbow
At the other end
Of our rainbow

We had only to
Fly just jet high
To get to the
Further end
Of our rainbow

Once we had
On land landed
Express bused
To a mission
Our rainbow's
Sun brightness
Revealed richness
Of our rainbow condition

There at the upper
Frisco art circle canyon
Where canvases
About their faces
In respect of
Our rainbow end arrival

Canvases that desire
Being silent
While creator He
Warmly welcomes us
To reside inside
His neat haven of Art

At this other end
Of our rainbow

After short
Greeting / talk while
He drives us
Through misson ways
Some mean streets
Strewn with
Misfortunate major
Women & men throughout
For some sum of
Those forgotten ones
Los Olvidados there
Is no rainbow
Beginning nor end
Their mission is
Merely their condition
Even crime
Does not pay
For their action
Nor their louder reaction
The only real rainbow
That los Olvidados
Does daily see
Is some multicolored
Flying cloths
Called gay flags

Nevertheless we
In pickup truck of He
Do indeed find
In Mission center
A needed divine
Rainbow end of
No pot-of-gold

But an enormous
Cornucopia of
Invigorating vegetables
Fresh fruit of tropic lands
And to augment
Our gourmet delight
The unexpected
Unfolds to our sight
Pancho Villa
Our patron horse riding
Passionate saint
A large fast self-service
Restaurant of good food
Bearing beloved
Pancho Villa's name

We enter this
Crowded eating place
He leads us to
Steaming counter
Of rainbow foodstuffs
Of rainbow reasonable prices

He orders for us
Speaking Mexicanamerican
To guapa señorita
Counter girl who
Cortez Conquistadors
Never dicktated
Her indio ancestors

This rainbow place
In Mission that
Restores our physical
Rainbow mental condition
We rejoice

Another again & again
Yellow arroz, frijoles
Negro plus Villa
Vegetables of green colors
Of our rainbow

He who paints
His brushes impregnated
Loaded heavy
With south of all borders
Bright sun shines
He of rainbow end
This He our friend
He was presenter
Of the other end
Of our rainbow
Mucho sol brother
Mucho hospitality
Mucho dream into reality
He who shared his rainbow

June 1997

Okapi Passion

dirty cuff links litter jungle floor
JUNGLE itself a Persian word
top hat hustlers tiger rag there
Afroid feature face film the
untaped toes dance until dark
the filthy "Etiquita Negra" feared
labels placed on Johnny The Talker
sexual harassed for perfidious
Okapi passion

thirty pairs of bushy caskets
cigarette coffin lid locked inside
nasty nicotine a rich Frenchman name
forest pianos tree cake walk
ultimately too tipsy to dip doodles
siren whisper concrete fire alert
inflammation spits spats matinee
tuxedo neck break of Caucasoid
Okapi passion

flirty palm tree shadows those
lindy hop skip the jumping joint
raincoated walrus women there
waller in bulbous fat buttocks
stage hands singe heifer hands
selected airpockets union picketed
hard off today hard hat tommorrow
Islamichebrew christian aroused
Okapi passion

thrifty   elegant   salsa rock quarry
dense wellbrushed scrotum musée
ballroom early helicopter bounce

first Mongoloid dust cut rug
cork condum stir riverboat emotion
paddle oval wheel until oar dance
open slowly younger fur fireplaces
tense teeth ballet step ladder
Okapi passion

shifty years get no anvil love
lust when pound weighed here
tram car care more on sheets
seals are sensual when frenched
lean redwoods to skyscrape there
both boogie woogie concerned
intellectualize male post persons
swift swamp waltz in Ituri for
Okapi passion

sift self-rising flower dick
broil steel beams until torn
microwave naked camera flash
in under museum muddy road
crosseyed while being hog fried
do the nut thang season squirrel
pay attention no odor demands
jelly roll blue jam can come to
Okapi passion

crafty worthy word monger
bebop spangled slider of banners
who but Bird could A-Train overtake
around about Tunisia nights
star dusty rule out dick tracers
neat three piece pussy catchers
bread basket of all   right   balls
Zaire   Zambia   Zimbabwe of
Okapi passion

elastic bloodcrank upward
tin overcoat well rusted
stone stench two step father
dance around not on the clock
ecstatic panties paint pitfalls
xylophone cold hard armpits
thimbles cancel condom laws
blue never fail climatic
Okapi passion

spastic complaint of vacuum glove
current screwdrivers to pick cotton
no bathrooms or bat women on planes
ask Antarctic banana zipper-upper
each wet response vaginal slippery
sweater perspire when swinging
kneel behind saxophone does
skin back beer hugging bus with
Okapi passion

aristocratic sleeping bag virgin
unfrocked each unfurled dawn
dry unarmchair child ink
deep cuddle cloud step dance
switch donkey task toward here
shake cattle of funky soul baby
lace up concrete foot tools now
prepare to maybe if perhaps in
Okapi passion

drafty eyelids of iron stove
offering pot belly below to all
suits fit to turn your damper down
tailor made grate kissed charcoal
crewcut flue jammed white soot
female sparks sprinkle cake legs

surely gangs of chains rhumba trot
Mexica Mali married Manhattan's
Okapi passion

certainly lipstick wearing originated there
amongst ancient prosperous prostitutes who
when menstrual time did impede vaginal need
radiant lips were advertised oral speed
early Egyptian invention to thus show
her painted lips allowed clients to know
However contemporary vacuum rubber caps
applied on platypus bills of high fasion
rites known now as Okapi passion

Mexico
12 December 1991

On Rue Jacques Callot

on rue Jacques Callot in Paris
a girl watches a man's pants fall
the sun flips like a tossed coin
and the girl licks her lips slow
on rue Jacques Callot in France

on this sunnyside street in Paris
a black flower first saw a Man Ray
and last saw Le Verre d'eau dans la Tempête
the naked beard makes sounds of dogs barking
on the rue Jacques Callot in Paris

on the rue Jacques Callot in Europe
where exquisite corpses drink no wines
the moon is pregnant with loud poems
and young whores knees lock against fever
on the rue Jaques Callot in France

on rue Jacques Callot on Left Bank
a flame thrower gives a taxi pillow
the water melon eater sucks a pussy cat
and four velvet pairs of panties swear
on the rue Jaques Callot in the Paris

Ouagadougou Ouagadougou

OUAGADOUGOU THELONIUS MONK SALUTES YOU

MUSICALLY   FROM AFROAMERICA

WITH HIS   EPISTROPHY

OUAGADOUGOU   OUAGADOUGOU   OUAGADOUGOU

OUAGADOUGOU

WHO SENT SURREALIST ME

TO EXPERIENCE YOU

THE   MOSSI   MANNERS   TO FETCH

ANCIENT BOBO   BIRD   MASK   OF

GREAT GRAND ANCESTORS   THOSE BLACK

DYNASTIES OF THE ANCIENT GLORIOUS PAST

OUAGADOUGOU   OUAGADOUGOU   OUAGADOUGOU

OUAGADOUGOU

THELONIUS MONK   AND SUN RA SALUTE YOU

BY TAKING OFF THEIR   AFROAMERICAN

LIDS   WHICH UNDER THEIR BARE

HEADS HAVE HID   UH HUH OUAGADOUGOU

THEY BOTH SALUTE YOU   OUAGADOUGOU!

Pills

I took my pill against
Malaria and washed it down
with well water now I have Typhoid again
I took my pill against
Pregnancy and washed it down
with sexy champagne now I'm having a baby
I took my pill against
Headache and washed it down
with good whiskey now I am drunk
I took my pill against
Malnutrition and washed it down
with fresh goat's milk now I got Hepatitis
I took my pill against
Headcold and washed it down
with a fine wine the combination made me blind
I took my pill against
Cramps and washed it down
with strong beer now I have acute diarrhea
I took my pill against
Fever and washed it down
with sparkling bottled water now I hiccup all day
I took my pill against venereal disease
and washed it down with a coke now I smell stronger
I took my pill against bigotry and hate and washed
it down with ox blood now vampire bats bother me
nightly

I took my pills/ the whole lot of them/ and washed
them down the toilet commode/ and flushed them/ now
my mind and body are in better condition/ here in a
pill box/ protected from all

Hellville, Noisse-Be, Malagasy
1982

194

Pre-Birth Memories
for S & P Cohen

To be inside your
Nine month pregnant
Cuntinent of mother
To look outside that
Glistening slit of joy
To be forewarned that
Cozy cuntinental
Residence stay was over
To begin to pack your
Few infantile belongings
And attempt to tidy up
Up the placid placenta place
To erase the intelligent
Graffiti off your mother's
Inner cuntinental walls
To sort through old and
Recent letters, faxes, etc.
Tossing most of it into the
Defecation bin or
Watery urinary wastebasket
To double check the
Time that reservation
Is assured in the
Outside of your
Mother's cuntinent
Onto the terrible
Polluted outside
To brace yourself
Like a parachutist's first jump
Like visiting a dentist first time
Like a virgin who has at last
Decided to take the very first fuck
To discard your childish

Fear of the unknown
To set yourself in the
Correct birth position
To rehearse your unique
Baby cry for breast
To prepare your umbilical
Cord to prevent
Umbilical strangulation
To take down your last
Inside confidential
Cuntinental notes
To memorize every
Inner activity including
Your fortunate father's
Sperm shot that
Your marvelous mother
Suprisingly fertilized
To realize
It is your birthtime
It is your unique countdown
You do an infant waterbreak
You shake, rattle and roll
Pop out into the unknown

Paris
4 July 1994

Pygmy Stay Away from My Door

Pygmy stay away from my door

the greasy grass has been combed
the large hairy eyebrow has been raised
the jealous husbands have come home
the mystic street walkers have slept
the money has been spent

Pygmy stay away from my door

Pygmy stay away from my door

the electric chair has blown a fuzz
the lightning has removed her clothes
the moon is naked and bright
the truck driver has learned to read and write
the rhinos roam through the hospital

Pygmy stay away from my door

Pygmy stay away from my door

the swinging swahili snores
the broom has crossed the street
the owls have flown near Nice
the widows have raped the postman
the brook has babbled at last

Pygmy stay away from my door

Pygmy stay away from my door

the blacks have raised a flag
the fleet has drowned a fish
the melon has never been stolen
the baby has become a circle
the umbrellas have covered a stone

Pygmy stay away from my door

Pygmy stay away from my door

the church is closed for angels
the hipster in America wails
the sweet Ukrainian whore sleeps
the awful Alabama girl aches
the nice Nubianegro tells time
the mean ol' Frisco blues are blown

So pygmy stay away from my door!

Rain & Rain

It is raining again
I just made it back
Into my cluttered
Paris pad of
Incognito

This creative crib
That I dwell in
When in Paris
Is across the hall
From a mattress thief
That is to say they
The loud Arab
And his louder lewd
French Fried woman she
Stole one of my mattresses

A week later
I gave them
My unfunctional bed
Now that I
Designed another bed
An elephant leg bed
Four & half feet
Above the dusty floor
When I look upon
My floor I sneeze
Asthmatic symptoms, you know

It is raining again
I was lucky
To make it up here
Where all is dry yet

Dusty too dusty
Almost like my
Other pad, a bigger one
Actually a house
In the ancient city
Of old Mali
Timbuktu, I'm telling you

Where I can be found
When some severe winters
Roar or roll around
No rain ever falls
Upon the sandy streets
And most of the water
Is the color I am

It is raining again
What a torrential downpour
Wind augmenting the rain
Visibility only a few feet
I saw many legs & feet
Multicolored they were
In Paolo Uccello's painting
At the overcrowded
Louvre Museum
The warriors bearing
More than 27 lances

And perhaps the most
Angry black horse in
All art history in the center
Its expression flashes
Like lightning
Its expression seems
To thunderously roar
And yet its rider
Has the harness slack

It is raining again
Heavy drops pouring fast
There are going to be
Many many wet people
Wringing their clothes out
Throughout Paris this night
Fortunately I am inside
Where I have seen
Old umbrellas

It is raining again
Somewhere else in
This big round universal world
Rain has no nationality
Rain could never be racist
And it is rain that brings
Good tidings, bad tidings
Or just a wet scene
For the dry & uncovered
Say hello to all rain wetly

It is raining again
Raining all hours
Throughout the world
Rain never prewarns you
Although gossipy thunder
Flashy flirtatious lightning &
Heavy dark brow clouds
Often assume rains en route
The first drops are the youngest
Unorganized

Paris

28 May 1992

Ready or Not
for Ed Clark

Certainly there are
One can believe that
Just as it is a fact
Of course there is no doubt
It really does exist
It is not so blatant
Yet it seriously prevails
There is no question
It is not quite overt
Nevertheless it is there
At readiness
However its manner
One must take care
Even during winter
Especially near dawn
When all is still
One must be careful
Caution must be exercised
Of course one could deny
That there are such
Believe it or not
It's really dangerous
For it does exist
It is an overt fact
No one intelligent denies it
No sane being questions it
It is a known fact
It is a proven fact
Basic above all
Nonetheless
There are those
One or two doubters

Who just cannot grasp it
And will not admit it *is* here
Even though they know
What we are talking about
It is right here
Ready to act

Gabon, Libreville
13 February 1994

Sans Subway

Bonjour Messieurs et
Mesdames, excusez-moi
Je suis, Je suis, Je suis
Sans l'argent sans adresse
Sans une femme sans famille
Sans chaussures, sans pantalon
Sans les gants sans chemise
Sans drapeau sans cadeau
Sans l'histoire sans passeport
Sans chapeau sans ratatouille
Sans aiguille sans pirogue
Sans gratte-ciel sans miel
Sans culotte because it is too hot!
Je suis sans Rock sans Roll
Sans Rap, Reggae et le Soul
Je suis, Je suis, Je suis
As your can see
Je suis nu, nu, nu
Merci
Au Revoir
Bonne nuit!

Paris Métro
21 May 1992

Sécurité

Fasten your trousers
To prevent your belt
From falling
Due to turbulence galore

Unload your knife
To protect your wife
From bullet patches
Due to loose slacks

Gather your own seeds
To plant wheelbarrows
From drought
Due to constipated rainfall

Mismanage your child care
To insure softer mattresses
From smoke stacking
Due to fast food fever

Well bake your clothespins
To block asthma seizures
From calling
Due to piano sexual tuning

Shake all airplane underwear
To destroy wheelbarrow seeds
From sprouting
Due to altitudinal changes

Crease all bracelet nostrils
To beautify vanity on trees
From winter on
Due to seasonal menopause

Carry all bags full of hands
To green washed rivers
From noon 'til midnight
Due to shortages

Lace quickly cloud smiles
To put forth the new law
From storm dandruffs
Due to fierce frownings

Disperse all taught thoughts
To intellectualize eyelid level
From published waters
Due to favorable breast watching

Drive straight metal breads
Onto menu video rebellions
Of mayonnaised film odors
Due to begin

Spurt spew or hand plow
To bouquet that prayer
From hand of cow mouth
Due to arrive on time

Detach any oat mill rotary
To increase rice paper speed
From ejaculation candidly
Due to coarse barley sneezes

Belch in B-flat upper floors
To cause bridges to fall forward
From young hinges
Due to puberty overflow

Assimulate tripod false teeth
To secretly sip molted lead
from vats of sifted lava lips
Due to burns of rainfall clouds

Security in all fifteen forms
Should be followed daily
To guarantee against
All forms of accidents that
Would lead to your death

Paris

22 May 1992

Shun Not This Rider

Penis ossification
Caused by you / okapi
Who walked barelegged
Toward a rose stem
That wanted so much
To be a barbwire's bride

Banjo classification
Caused by you / aardvark
Growing a lovely lawn
That could be mown
Beneath your navel's frontyard
Until I plucked-plunked it

Cornbread mastication
Caused by you / tapir
Who tongueless talked
On rumbled foreskin beds
Between lowering helicopters
Erecting hammocks by heart

Armpit demystification
Caused by you / rhinoceros
Dancing a black butter smear
Dictionary female needs
Base stealing unwashed machines
That dream of being a razor
In crouched gambler's gear

Zootsuit eradication
Caused by you / pangolin
Who deliberately come first
Showering ceilings with sparks
Rolling out the dark stout barrels
Until overcrowded deserts sunk

Saxophone education
Caused by you / puffin bird
Jazz blasting square edges off
Naked mothers seen obvious
Spreading truth amongst needy
Now trees grow upside round

Jelly roll glorification
Caused by you/giraffe
Opening such a sane circle
In full summer sun set view
A blazing saddle of my desire
No contentment without that cuntinent

Suspenders putrefacation
Caused by you / zebra
Shadowing her box of goodies
Plain black on white nitty-gritty
A suction cap of feminine resources
Until the door bails out I strip . . . your body

Vaginal insinuation
Caused by you / porcupine
Creating awesome images on quills
Blankets bent back and ready
A trusted thrust of countdowns
No clatter of clitoridecto/my here . . . your now

Trumpet calculation
Caused by you / platypus
Who boogie-woogied across eyes
Nude duckbill and paid for
Pot smoking on electric stoves
Embracer of male and female sex . . . your claoca!

See Circuit Rider, See What We Done Done!

24 April 1978

Smoke Sleep
to Étienne Léro

I am smoking like horse on fire, a fire hose / sick car / or cigarette
In Paris/Port au Prince/I the Black Prince / smoking menthol cool / calm
As tropical rain forest shadows / trees proud and naked / more natural nude
I have never seen a tree dressed / although I have blown a shoehorn / loud
At the very bottom / of shoe laces / snake with head at each end / or
      beginning
I am smoking / nearby Jardins Luxembourg / and Congo Basin /
crowded
      with trees
That have Sex with young under-age / papillons surrealists / butterflies,
No more/British slanted buttocks / dressed for tenor / a saxophoned yesterday
I have an enormous / hard-off, for dialing / reporting my coat / drowning in
The Sahara Ocean / just below oil / Dinner teeth sharpened / spadelike digger
I wear no false feet / false head gear / frost eyelashes / backlashes of
Niggertine stain / fixed Dixieland grin / Remembering Pearl Harbor / bitch!!
I am smoking / call the Frying man / my pan is running over / car blamed
I have an ancient broom / for sale, cleans dirty / fulla rum in Paris morn
They made him, he is wooden / but willing / unlike the steaming
      shovel / broke
Kilimanjaro is my bride/she has her sex / on the Left / red green as black
Smoke wets our crying / tears fear cigars / washed by Mandarin-Curasa shot
Tease her twice before stripping / tobacco plant / a spy no doubt / call Holm
Dial all phones backwards / graffiti fit festival / Freudlike Coltraning
On your rue Tournon / nearby I smoking / Damas told me a bit / whale
      wailer
Another France / same Africa / another Martinique / same French paw,
      scratching
Ce n'est pas moi / I am smiling / giraffe witnesses / volcano ominous / terse?
Under a minute skirt / jacket fuming / furious is forest / hairy as breath / broth
Left over Karl defeated / new African Samba-Conga-Mamba-Chacha /
      git-a-way
Erection before cat food / the breasts of top coats / await nothing / white

I smoking / circles curl under blankets, smoke is noisy / igloo spooky / sniff
Leave money / on dotted line / Chemin-de-fer wears under / painting
     for cul
Causing a coup-d'état / dat ain't be working / Smoke rangs rocking /
     dance gal
Funky forks / memory of lost chapter / autobiog orgy boot / match
     book read
Dusty bowls of soap beans / break-yr-fast / a tropical failure trunk / sic?
I am smoking for you / mon ami / pour toi

So Fortunately Unfortunately

When in written
English or American
I can thus find
A poem that does
Not at all use:
The, of, and, to, a, in,
That, is, I, it, for
And of course "as"
Nor does such
A rare poem ever rhyme
It is then
In awe
I shall softly wheeze
The often used
African word
W   O   W !

Rabat, Morocco
16 January 1989

Spent Penny

lick my shopping carts
limbs with rusty tongue
on rue de la femme sans tête
sur rue de la femme cent têtes
i loose a penny not by choice
it flipped out of my pocket
giraffe necked the hell away
copped out from pocketed okapi
ended as the "z" in zebra
although laundered sheets know
zebra begins with "z" but
zebra ends with "a"
rare thoughts of penny stove
a letuce would be chewed food
i choose sunday to say:
penny spent!
that is unworthy of she/me
better to settle such an affair
like hummingbird in bush
without locked underwear
limping carts support my tongue
no pat on the back can help
i cry a shy goodbye
in key of z
on rue de la femme sans tête
on rue de la femme sans ted
this penny that spent me

Paris
2 May 1976

Tant Pis!

to Ms. Jenny Searle of Exeter

to YOUR . . .
your head full of jellybeans
your skull of hard wax
your face filled with fear
your figure of water shape
your hair of wine tears
your cheeks painted with wool
your neck wrapped in soap bubbles
your bust exploded backwards pink
your chest full of hot charcoals
your breast bright with coffin nails
your spine drenched with orgasm dew
your left side weighted in oats
your right side weighted in rye waves
your hips too dumb to swing black
your belly sunk from farted funk
your heart hid inside a bent tampon
your artery solid as marbles on move
your veins split to spit out mosquitoes
your pulse purrs like a winter fire
your blood of material gains pressure
your brain of sewage and drain pipes
your nerves of frightful noons and midnights
your wrinkles that fold in their itches
your skin of blue jean and body butter
your flesh of concrete and foreskins
your muscle that coughs tar babies
your bones of shredded flames of fog
your joints coated in ashes of hinges
your skeleton under combs of bread
your eyes of scary delights
your ears filled with horrow and hard ones

your nose stink of the fox tails
your mouth of merry-go-rounds
your lips that explode Exeter
your tongue covered in crime
your teeth coated with whale navel dust
yourt arms bent with wetness
your elbows backwards as lies
your hands as guilty as amerikkkans
your fingers sprinkled in belts
your legs folded on typewriters
your knees flown across giraffes
your ankles functional as history
your toes stuck to anvil rectums
your lungs loaded with flies
your saliva sewn with barbed wire
your stomach bloated with truth
your liver hanging on a blue barn
your kidney causes steam coats
your intestines filled with book covers
your buttocks resemble all that I love
your face imitates everything that is bad
I the Bitchdoctor

15 March 1972

The Enigma of Francis Parrish of Paris France

Under the cold bed I saw
heavy masses of shadows and many people of all races

ready to fall on the sleeping knife and the snoring plate
happy as I shall be to see this uncanny sight

The oceanlike landscape that no one dares to tread on
only the giant form Macy's dares to leave imprints in its surface

Under the hot frosted bed I saw
a mangled trumpet that Dizz never blew and never wished to

the sound of a crushed baby filled the ears of all horses and toothpicks
happy as I shall be to see this and to even listen to this uncanny happen

"Understanding the rights of an artist is for God and not for man"
said the fleur de lis to the floating image

Under the fleshy filled bed I saw
all the important dreamscapes and multi-colored people

they were all awaiting my signal to place the crown upon the head of the
queen of all dreams his dreams your dreams their dreams they were
waiting and happy to assist in such a ceremony

the stones were no longer hard they were soft as Camembert cheese and
even the image that defied all explanation became almost explicable

Under the empty glass bed I saw
the queen rise into the air with her magic Celtic scandals

her knees were close together and they were no longer knees but were
amphibious nuns saying a prayer for mercy on the apache that had
blown the trademarks of France away and were now awaiting their
sentence

Queen Francis de Parrish with hands gracefully folded smiled and said
"Blessed is the tin can that doeth no harm to the bare foot that treadeth it"
Under the bloody lung-filled bed I had seen
Under the bloody toothpick I had tasted
Under the bloody bass drum I had listened
Under the sugar-coated maggot I had crawled for a better view
of the dreamscape which the coronation played to the important role
in your soul his soul their soul and even the shoe soul

cosmic rays have penetrated

16 April 1953

The Hat

it sits there
it sits right over there
it sits there alone and proud
it sits over there waiting for a head
it always gets a head
it was made for getting a head
it must be musical with its band
it is one of the best
it is always covering up
it is forever non square
it cannot be worn on the ass
it can be understood by all
it has fought with the elements
it is my hat
it is my hat that you've hung
it is my hat that is guilty
it is my hat that runs away with the wind
it is my hat your broadbutt sits upon
it is my hat that is left on the rack
it is my hat from everywhere
it is my hat that is tipped
it is my hat that talks to my brain
it is my hat that is my crown
it is my hat   it is my hat   it is my hat   it is
                        my hat IT IS MY HAT!!
    oh hell—I'm wearing my cap!

The Overloaded Horse

On a battu le cheval, au mois de Mai and they ate him
his buttons were crushed into powder for their soup
  his hair was woven into ship sails
his foreskin was sewn by an antique dealer
his manure supplied several generations with xmas gifts
  and now they speak bad of him, the horse, the head of their family
  On a battu le cheval, au mois de Mai and they ate him
  his earwax was packaged in America
his rump was displayed on early morning garbage trucks
  his crossed eye is on loan to a soap museum
  his manners have since been copied by millions of glass blowers
  and still yet, they spit at his stable, the horse, the head of the house
  On a battu le cheval, au mois de Mai and they ate him
his ribs were riveted outside an airbase
his knees bend in shadows of Russia
  his shoelaces are used to hang lonely violinists
his dignity is exported as a dairy product to the Orient
  and in spite of it all, those he loves most, lie and cheat horse's heirs
  On a battu le cheval, au mois de Mai and they ate him
  his tears now drown the frowning yachtsmen
his urine flows rapidly across millionaires' estates
his annual vomit destroys twelve dictators' promises a year
his teeth tear wide holes in the scissor maker's Swiss bank account
  and even in death, filled with revenge, they eat him again and again
  they deny and lie as they speak bad of the horse, the head of their
  house, the father of their home

The Statue of 1713

The statue of André Breton
stands at Tanezrouft Trail's end
the pedestal on which it stands
made of marvelous owl wings from Mali
gives off artificial lighting
accompanied by Tuareg war shouts
The author of *Nadja* is scupted nude
by five or fifteen Africans (fetish makers!)
I am not quite certain of how many they are
even though some wear numbered miners' caps
occupied by their serious structuring
these fetish makers do not realize the cold
the cold comes creeping out of the darkness
from the Sahara where it had buried itself
during the heat of the day
the cold has always been the enemy of the sun
They both once worked for a black Jesus in a
carpenter shop (the sun quit first!)
Afterwards a blue Jesus froze and rose
The statue of André Breton
stands on a huge granite rock that
tumbled up from Adrar des Iforhas
those black buttocked mountains where
no fennecs live
The pedestal of Malian owl wings is weeping
causing showers of electric sparks to fall
on the sand surrounding that noble statue
Desert bandits on muzzled mouth camels and
armed with Congolese openers and Tanzanian soaps
steer their dangerous gangs
in the opposite directions
they fear the truth of that poet

in this remote part of erg and reg Sahara
The statue of André Breton
is taller than forty-two giraffes' necks
and wider than a street of fountain pens
an ancient poster from Montmarte
serves as a rug for the chief fetisher
He who hacks fast as quicksilver with his adze
the other fetish brothers work slower
since their work is to make detail and decorate
Those few that wear Tombouctou gold around
their penis and scrotum are entrusted to
translate the surrealist manifestos into
Tamachek thus enabling one to read them
backwards as well as forwards
One Senoufo fetisher covered with ivory
form the coast sees the Dogon night train
hurling and howling through the night
or is it a giant female sand viper angered
by donkey's dung drying near her fat eggs?
One cannot be positive it is not her!
The desert like a metropolis is full of mirages
The statue of André Breton
leans toward the East ignoring the West
both thumbs pointing outward
signifying faith in the South and North
A trio of ragged ostriches trot across
the clouds blotting out those holes
in the black sky—called Bobo stairs or
Bayaka stars—I pull my mosquito net up to allow
Maldoror a chance to enter my bed
He is a hairy tarantula tonight
He points his stolen octopus tentacle
at the plaque on the pedestal of André Breton
I read the inscription that Maldoror
had written: THE WHITE HAIRED REVOLVER
IS STILL LOADED!

A shudder ran through my mistress
she who had hidden under the mattress
(Maldoror was never a lover of women)
I bid him good night with a baseball bat
He winged off into the desert as a glass bat with
fog lights
The statue of André Breton
a vertical sphinx in this sea of sand
created from one sacred baobab tree
brought up from Haute Volta on the heads
of female volunteers (all pregnant with
poets' babies!)
Strong females of all nations and notions
from Tennessee and Togo, Tinchebray and Tangier
they came bearing the gigantic tree
The fetishers and I witnessed their coming
the tree was left on a bed of ribbons
ribbons of colors that would shame a rainbow
I witnessed the women's noisy retreat at the
approach of the masked fetishers
Their drums spoke flames and thunder
frightening a white stallion 1,413
kilometers away
trumpets roared black waves of sound
flutes screamed and accused asthma
the sun in all its glory spun wildly
the statue of André Breton
stands in the shadow of no others
yet casting its own long distant intelligent
shadow into hands, hearts and minds
of men
This immense statue created by fetishers
festooned with gri-gri from home
and abroad stands as a living piece
of sculpture (a poem)

an awesome magnetic monument
for the beautiful women and
brilliant men
that felt the
presence of André Breton!

en route Tenerife
5 March 1967

The Sun My Son

dedicated to the first woman I ever slept with, my mother

if only the sun would shine to   night

the   m o o n   would   seem   twice brighter

if only the sun would shine   tonight

white boy you'd   seem   w h i t e r

purple cows
pulling golden plows
through   a marshy   toilet

woolen brassieres
wornout by years
pink   light red   and   scarlet

if only the sun would shine tonight

the   moon   could   sleep   til   morning

if   only   the   sun   would shine   tonight

there   would   never   be   no   d a w n i n g

They Rode Hyenas during the Night

to Jorge Camacho

THEY RODE HYENAS IN A FIERY SQUARE

THEIR HYENAS BLEED FIRE

THEIR HYENAS' MOUTHS DRIP   ICE COLD VOMIT

THEY RODE HYENAS   NAKED

THEIR FEET BECAME SMOOTHING IRONS

THEIR BUTTOCKS GLISTENED AS THOUGH MIRRORS

THEIR HAIR WAS BURNING BUSHES

THEY RODE THEIR FIERY SQUADRON NORTH

THEY SWOOPED DOWN OUR CAMPSITE

THEIR HYENAS' RAZOR MOUTHS CUT US

THEY STOMPED US WITH IRON FEET

THEY SET OUR HEARTS AND SOULS ON FIRE

THEIR HYENAS TORE OUT OUR INTESTINES

THEY SAT THEIR BUTTOCKS ON OUR FACES

THEY SMOTHERED US WITH WHITE HOT MIRROR

THEIR HYENAS' FOAM FROZE OUR BREATH

THEY LEFT US AT DAWN

THEY HAD MADE US LIKE THEM

30 December 1977

To Be What / Is Not To Be

IF

WHEN

WHY
    IF
    WHAT
    WHERE
IF

WHO WAS
    THEN

    WHY

    WHEN
IF

WHERE

WHAT

IF

WHO

WERE
    THERE

    WAS

Untitled

There are those whom
Humans chose
As not to have
An expiration date
in their infinitesimal passport
Here on earth

So when
One of those
Instantly do die
We humans are surprised
Filled immediately
With sincere grief

And wonder why
Could sudden death
Or any form of death
Stop the life
Of those we've chose
To forever live
And we love
Gone,
But never to be
Forgotten

No bye bye

5 August 1999

The Truth

IF YOU SHOULD SEE A   MAN

walking down a crowded

street
  talking
      ALOUD

TO HIMSELF

      DON'T RUN
           IN THE

OPPOSITE DIRECTION

          BUT RUN

TOWARD HIM

    for he is a

        POET

you have NOTHING to
          FEAR

FROM THE

    POET
      BUT THE

  TRUTH

Printed in the USA
CPSIA information can be obtained
at www.ICGtesting.com
JSHW022320140824
68134JS00019B/1214